Chaim Weizmann

Makers
of the
Modern
World

Chaim Weizmann
The Zionist Dream
T G Fraser

HH
HAUS HISTORIES

First published in Great Britain in 2009 by
Haus Publishing Ltd
70 Cadogan Place
London SW1X 9AH
www.hauspublishing.com

Copyright © T G Fraser, 2009

The moral right of the author has been asserted

A CIP catalogue record for this book
is available from the British Library

ISBN 978-1-905791-67-5

Series design by Susan Buchanan
Typeset in Sabon by MacGuru Ltd
Printed in Dubai by Oriental Press
Maps by Martin Lubikowski, ML Design, London

Contents

Acknowledgements   vi
Preface   viii

I The Life and the Land   1
1 From the Pale of Settlement to the Pursuit of Zion   3
2 Palestine under the Ottomans   21
3 War and the Balfour Declaration   36

II The Paris Peace Conference   65
4 The Paris Peace Conference   67

III The Legacy   95
5 San Remo, the National Home and Arab resistance   97
6 Weizmann: the prisoner of Zion?   123

Notes   147
Chronology   168
Further Reading   183
Bibliography   188
Picture Sources   195
Index   197

Acknowledgements

I am grateful to the Series Editor, my friend and colleague Professor Alan Sharp, for reawakening a long-standing interest in Chaim Weizmann's career. Although I have returned to the Middle East many times since, my first visit a quarter of a century ago was to the Weizmann Archives in Rehovoth when I was researching a study of partition, and I have retained the memory of the kindly welcome I received there. Jaqueline Mitchell of Haus Publishing patiently answered my many questions as the project unfolded. Professor Gillian Robinson, Director of the University of Ulster's International Conflict Research (INCORE), provided a congenial and stimulating academic home when I retired from the university. Janet Farren deployed her customary skills in preparing my work for the publisher. In the midst of all the other priorities of academic life, my colleague Dr Leonie Murray willingly and patiently read through my typescript with a fine critical eye, saving me from many errors of expression and emphasis. My wife, Grace, roamed the Internet to find books and pamphlets which provided many invaluable insights into Weizmann's career, and also refined my prose in the light of her own experience of the Middle East. I hope they all approve the final result, but any errors are my own.

T G Fraser

Professor Emeritus of History and Honorary Professor of Conflict Research, University of Ulster

July 2008

Preface

When Chaim Weizmann presented himself before the representatives of the principal victorious Allied and Associated Powers at the Peace Conference in Paris on 27 February 1919 it marked a decisive moment in what had, thus far, been an extraordinary career which had taken him from one of the more obscure parts of Europe to the heart of international diplomacy. When he died at home in Rehovoth on 9 November 1952, he was President of the newly established State of Israel, the first Jewish polity in their ancient homeland since the time of their dispersion at the hands of the Romans almost 2,000 years earlier. At the time of his birth on 27 November 1874 in Motol, then part of the Tsarist empire and now in Belarus, the situation of the Jews could not have been more starkly different.

This book makes no claim to re-tell every aspect of Weizmann's long and varied career, still less is it a study of the origins of the Israeli-Palestinian question. Rather, its focus is on the critical period before, during and after the Peace Settlement when Weizmann was at the centre of complex diplomatic moves which led to the establishment of the British Mandate for Palestine committed to pursuing the Balfour Declaration in favour of the creation of a Jewish National Home, without which the events leading to the creation of Israel and the consequent Israeli-Palestinian problem would have been very different, perhaps non-existent. When set against the critical issues in Europe and elsewhere which the peacemakers had to address in the aftermath of the First World War, the future of Palestine may have seemed of marginal importance, and Weizmann's presentation before them over in a matter of minutes; but the far-reaching consequences of what he said and did there more than justify such a study in a series of volumes on the Peace Conference and its legacies.

Given the Conference's significance, it was inevitable that all manner of groups would want to come to Paris to try their luck, as Ireland's Sinn Fein did without success. That the Zionists were able to do so, was in no small measure the result of Weizmann's carefully calibrated campaign in the highest reaches of British politics throughout the war. This ensured that their voice was heard in Paris by men who were familiar with the Jewish case over Palestine, and who had sympathised with it. The Arabs of Palestine enjoyed no such platform. As their fears over British and Zionist intentions mounted, they turned instead to political mobilisation on the ground, something which Weizmann had begun to sense as early as the spring of 1918, and which British officers in Palestine were tracking even before the Conference ended. The contest over the future of Palestine was starting to take shape. Ninety years after the Conference, what Weizmann said and did there is an essential part of our understanding of how this small, but critical, part of the world evolved out of its deliberations.

A HAPPY

NEW YEAR!

לשנה טובה

Leaders of the Zionist movement before the First World War.
(Top row, left to right) Nahum Sokolow, Chaim Weizmann.
(Centre) Theodore Herzl.
(Bottom row, left to right) Max Nordau, Ahad Ha'am.

I

The Life and the Land

1

From the Pale of Settlement to the Pursuit of Zion

If we accept the wisdom of Wordsworth that the Child is father of the Man, then it is to Motol and the Jewish Pale of Settlement in Russia that we must turn. At the time of Weizmann's birth in 1874, the Tsarist Empire, which had acquired much of Poland in the late 18th century, held the largest Jewish population in the world. From 1772 onwards, the Jews were compelled to live in the western parts of the empire in an area designated the Jewish Pale. While many of them lived in cities like Vilnius, Odessa and Warsaw, or in large towns like Pinsk, many others grouped together in small towns known in Yiddish, the *lingua franca* of Eastern Europe's Jews, as *shtetls*. Motol was just such a *shtetl*, and it shaped the first 11 years of Weizmann's life. Apart from its two synagogues, it had little of what later generations would term amenities. But by the standards of the Pale at that time, Weizmann's family enjoyed a decent, if modest, lower middle class way of life. Their home had a kitchen and seven rooms, and its adjoining land provided the family with fruit, vegetables and milk. Ozer Weizmann, Chaim's father, was engaged in the timber trade, the mainstay of the local economy, employing men to cut logs which were then tied into rafts and floated down the rivers Pina, Bug and Vistula to Danzig, as modern Gdansk was then called, on the Baltic. He was well respected, widely read, and sufficiently devout to serve as a prayer leader, or *Chazan*, in the more prestigious of the community's two synagogues. Rachel Leah, Ozer's wife, had 15 children, of whom 12 survived into maturity. Chaim was her third.[1]

If the Weizmann household was comfortable by the standards of the time, it was only won at the price of hard work on the part of Ozer and Rachel Leah, and in the knowledge that for the Jews life in the Pale could always be precarious. From the age of four until he was 11, Chaim Weizmann attended *cheder*, the little schools which provided instruction in Hebrew and the Jewish Law and Scripture. While he seemingly had no high opinion or kindly memory of some of his teachers, they embedded in him a profound sense of his own Jewish identity, reinforcing the atmosphere he absorbed at home.[2] Although he was to outgrow his origins, the values of Russian Jewry were to be the essential element in his later devotion to Zionism, setting him apart from, and often at odds with, some of the most prominent Jewish figures in Western Europe and the United States. This sense of where he was grounded comes across vividly in his first surviving letter, written in 1885 to Shlomo Sokolovsky, his tutor in the Russian language, which he needed to acquire to advance his education. Weizmann was concerned to reassure him that he would not abandon Judaism, and expressed his ardent support for the new *Hibbat Zion* (Love of Zion) movement which saw Palestine as offering the Jews a future. Interestingly, in view of the central role it was to assume in his life, he mentioned England, a country which he could only have imagined, as the one European state which would look favourably on the Jews.[3]

The movement which had aroused the young Weizmann's ardour was founded in 1882; its adherents known as *Hovevei Zion* (The Lovers of Zion). It was essentially a response to renewed persecution of the Jews in the Tsarist empire, and, despairing of assimilation, its members looked instead to Palestine. In November 1884, their first conference was held at Kattowitz, just across the border in Prussian Silesia. Weizmann's letter shows that he was aware of their idealism, but also of the circumstances which were spurring them into action. Anti-Semitism had been on the increase in the empire, stoked by its political and economic problems and the growth of Slavophile sentiments, but what gave it new impetus was the assassination in St Petersburg in March 1881 of Alexander II the 'Tsar Liberator', so called on account of his emancipation of the serfs, albeit in a manner which did not much benefit them. Of the six revolutionaries convicted of the murder, one was a young Jewish woman, Khasia Helfman. This event served to unleash a series of pogroms, as anti-Jewish riots were known, which began soon after the coronation of Alexander III and swept across areas as far apart as Warsaw and Odessa. Then, on 3 May 1882, the 'May Laws' were enacted which placed the Jews of the empire under even more severe restrictions than they had so far endured. Increasingly marginalised within the empire, hundreds of thousands of Jews emigrated, some across the border to the more tolerant Habsburg lands, others further afield to Britain, and, especially, to the United States. Between 1882 and the outbreak of war in 1914, some 2.6 million Russian Jews migrated to America, most of them to New York. Such was the grim reality behind the happy Weizmann household in Motol.

It was then, armed with a growing knowledge of Russian to add to his Yiddish and Hebrew, that Weizmann left Motol to begin his secondary education at the *Real-Gymnasium* in Pinsk, some 25 miles away. Two things stand out from his time there, each of which was to mould his subsequent career. Few things can be as inspirational in a young life as a schoolmaster or schoolmistress with talents beyond the ordinary and so it proved with Weizmann, since his interest in science, and chemistry in particular, was captured and fostered by a teacher called Kornienko. With a small laboratory at his disposal and a kindly manner, Kornienko set Weizmann on the academic course which was to be the lodestone of his subsequent path as an eminent scientist.[4]

Of even greater significance for the future were Weizmann's contacts with Pinsk's large and varied Jewish community, since Jews were a majority of the town's population, with a wider social and educational mix than anything he had so far encountered in Motol. The town's professional and business classes were strongly assimilationist, but amongst Jews of Weizmann's social background the new *Hibbat Zion* movement had taken hold. Its local leader was Rabbi David Friedman, who had been a leading figure at the Kattowitz conference. As Kornienko had done with chemistry, Friedman clearly fired the adolescent Weizmann, who worshipped in the synagogue attached to his house, and in the evenings plodded the streets of Pinsk raising money for the cause. Such was his introduction to the nascent Zionist movement with which his name was to become indelibly linked.[5] Although he was later to become somewhat dismissive of Pinsk, that was with the experience of a great city like Berlin behind him.[6] Unprepossessing and drearily provincial Pinsk might have been, but it was shaping him just the same.

At the age of 19, Weizmann decided to pursue his higher education in Germany. This move was not surprising given Germany's reputation in science and technology, but more important was the fact that if he remained in Russia he would have to battle against the *numerus clausus*, the system which restricted the percentage of Jews entering university. His opportunity came when he was offered a part-time position as teacher of Hebrew and Russian at a leading Jewish boarding school at Pfungstadt. His stipend, augmented by his allowance from home, enabled him to enrol for classes at the university in nearby Darmstadt. It was evidently a miserable time for him. He was homesick, poorly fed, and repelled by the prevailing assimilationism of the German Jews he encountered. After two terms, he returned home in poor health. If Darmstadt had been an acute disappointment, an upturn in his father's business affairs enabled him to enrol at the prestigious Charlottenburg *Polytechnikum* in Berlin in 1893.[7] Apart from a break back in Pinsk in 1895–6, Weizmann studied in Berlin until 1897 when he followed his mentor, Professor Bystrzycki, to the University of Fribourg in Switzerland, from which he graduated with his doctorate *magna cum laude* in 1899. He now had the credentials needed to follow an academic career in chemistry, which he began as a *Privat Dozent*, which carried no formal salary but was the vital first step, at the University of Geneva. His personal fortunes also underwent a significant change since he became engaged to a medical student from Russia, Sophia Getzova, though this attachment was not fated to last very long.[8]

If his studies in Berlin had set him on an academic path which was in time to mark him out as a scientist of international reputation, these coincided with other events which were to have infinitely greater significance for his place in

Jewish history. Zionism had no single point of origin. The Jews were too widely dispersed, and their situations too different, for that. Although ideas of political action began to surface amongst Jewish intellectuals in the 19th century, the term itself appears to have been used first by the Austrian Nathan Birnbaum in April 1890 in his journal *Selbstemanzipation*. 'Zion' referred, of course, to Jerusalem. Although he created the term 'Zionism', Birnbaum was to part company from it later. Nevertheless, his ideas anticipated those of another Viennese who is regarded as the real father of modern Zionism, Theodore Herzl, or in Hebrew, Benyamin Ze-ev Herzl.[9]

ASSIMILATIONISM
The 19th century saw Jews advance into prominent positions in various European countries. Some of them were converts to Christianity, for example, the German composer Felix Mendelssohn, the British economist David Ricardo and the statesman Benjamin Disraeli, Earl of Beaconsfield. Others held to their Jewish faith, asserting that they were a religious community like the Catholics, Anglicans or Lutherans. It was from the assimilationist Jews that some of the most determined opposition to Zionism came, as Weizmann discovered in the case of Edwin Montagu, Secretary of State for India.

Herzl's origins were in the German-speaking Jewish middle class of the Habsburg Empire. He was born on 2 May 1860 in the city of Pest, which in 1872 united with its twin across the Danube to become Budapest, the capital of the Hungarian part of the empire. In 1878, he became a law student at the University of Vienna, then one of the most culturally vibrant cities in Europe, albeit one in which anti-Semitism was beginning to stir and which he was to encounter as a student. Although he gained employment as a state lawyer, his real ambitions lay in literature, and while he struggled to have his plays accepted he found his niche, that of a writer of feuilletons for the press. These were short, finely-crafted pieces much prized by educated Viennese, and in 1888 he was engaged to write them for the *Wiener Neue Freie Presse*, the capital's leading newspaper.

Two things conspired to change Herzl's essentially assimilationist position. The first was the growing success in Viennese municipal politics of the Christian Social Party led by Dr Karl Lueger. Lueger, who was prepared to espouse anti-Semitism to advance his party's fortunes, was elected Lord Mayor of Vienna in 1895, and although the Emperor Franz Josef refused three times to confirm him, such was his popularity that he assumed the office in 1897, holding it until his death in 1910. Adolf Hitler was later to extol his virtues in *Mein Kampf*. If confirmation were needed of the rising tide of anti-Semitism in Europe, then Herzl received it as Paris correspondent for his newspaper at the time of the Dreyfus affair in 1894–5. Captain Alfred Dreyfus, an assimilated Jew, was convicted, wrongly as it was later shown, of selling military secrets to Germany. On 5 January 1895, Herzl witnessed the formal degradation of Dreyfus in the courtyard of the *École Militaire* in Paris. What particularly appalled Herzl about this miserable spectacle was the crowd outside chanting 'Death to the Jews'.[10] The success of Lueger's party in March 1895 further exposed the degree of anti-Semitism in two of Europe's most sophisticated cities, Paris and Vienna, and set the scene for the book Herzl was to publish the following year.

His book, or rather pamphlet, was published in Vienna and Leipzig on 14 February 1896. It had the somewhat ponderous title of *Der Judenstaat, Versuch einer modernen Lösung der Judenfrage*, normally rendered in English as *The Jewish State, An Attempt at a Modern Solution of the Jewish Question*, though a more accurate translation would be *The Jews' State*. Based on his recent dismal experiences in Vienna and Paris, his premise was essentially the pessimistic one that the pursuit of assimilationism was a false trail. The fact that Jews had given their loyalty to and had tried to enrich their countries through their contributions to the economy, art and science had been in vain. The history of anti-Semitism, he went on to argue, had made the Jews into a people who could make a state. He foresaw the need for an organisation to work towards this, proposing a Society of Jews which would prepare the way and a Jewish Company which would carry the project forward. There were two possible locations for such a state. The first was Argentina, which he argued had plenty of good land and a small population. The other was their historic homeland of Palestine. If that were to be granted by the Ottoman Sultan, it could become an outpost of Western civilisation. Such was the essence of his book, which went on to describe the future state in romantic, not to say visionary, terms. The idea of a Jewish state, and an organisation to bring it into being, had entered the public domain.[11]

For many, perhaps most, assimilationist Jews of Western and Central Europe, Herzl's book was opening up issues about anti-Semitism which they had hoped was becoming a thing of the past. In the winter of 1896/7, Herzl nevertheless worked single-mindedly to put his ideas into effect. His efforts culminated in the first Zionist Congress at Basel in Switzerland in August 1897. A seemingly modest affair of 197 delegates, it was historic, and the programme it approved was brief and to the point. The purpose of Zionism was to secure a home for the Jews in Palestine. In order to achieve this, Jews were to be encouraged to settle there, an organisation was to be created, Jewish national sentiment was to be fostered, and government consent secured.[12] The achievement of the Zionist programme might have seemed a distant dream, but the essential first step had been taken. While Herzl was well aware that Zionism had to negotiate with the Ottoman rulers in Constantinople, whose writ ran in Palestine, notably absent from his analysis, then and later, were the Arabs of Palestine.

Where was Weizmann in all of this? To his later chagrin, he was not present at Basel, but that did not mean that during his time in Berlin he was not fully caught up in these events nor watching them with keen interest. There is a symmetry between his progress in Pinsk and that in Berlin. In the former, he had been inspired by Kornienko and Friedman, whereas in Berlin if Bystrzycki fostered his scientific development, his evolution as a Zionist was in no small measure the result of his association with the writer and philosopher Asher Zvi Ginsberg, who had adopted the name Ahad Ha'am, 'One of the People'. Weizmann wrote in his autobiography that he was to Zionist students like himself what Mazzini had been to Young Italy.[13] While Weizmann was to develop a marked talent for quarrelling with his fellow Zionists, Ahad Ha'am, who died in Tel Aviv in 1927, was not one of them. However, unlike Herzl, actually having visited Palestine in 1891, Ahad Ha'am knew that the Arabs would not readily surrender to the Zionists, and sounded a warning to that effect.[14]

Weizmann's view of *Der Judenstaat* was that it contained nothing that was original, and that it ignored the work of others, like Birnbaum. There was certainly truth in this, but he also conceded that what gave the book its force was the personality of its author. Herzl's unique gift to Zionism was the fact that he moved from writing the book, which could have become no more than a historical curiosity, to organising and inspiring the first Zionist Congress. Weizmann should have attended this as a delegate from Pinsk, but that year his father's business fortunes declined, and he decided to travel to

Moscow in an attempt, unsuccessful as it turned out, to sell a dyestuff formula he had developed. Moscow, of course, was technically barred to him as lying outside the Pale, and the difficulties he encountered made him late for the Congress.[15]

He was able to make up for this absence at the Second Zionist Congress at Basel in 1898, and from then on was a regular attender and participant. During this time he made the acquaintance of the leading Russian Zionist, Menahem Mendel Ussishkin, an early member of *Hibbat Zion* who had been born in 1863. Over the years this gifted, if sometimes turbulent, man was to become a key collaborator of Weizmann, joining him in the presentation to the Paris Peace Conference, though the two parted company over the issue of partition in the late 1930s, shortly before Ussishkin's death in 1941.[16] Weizmann began to make his mark at the Fifth Zionist Congress in 1901 on a subject which was to capture his imagination, education, and in particular the concept of a Jewish university. Given the disabilities of young Jews under the Russian *numerus clausus*, and the fact that not everyone could afford to study in Western Europe, the idea of establishing a Jewish university was a matter of considerable importance, and it pre-dated Weizmann's involvement. Even so, his close interest and involvement were evident. In December 1901, a Youth Conference, largely inspired by Weizmann, led to the establishment of a group within Zionism known as the Democratic Faction. At the Fifth Zionist Congress which took place immediately after, the Democratic Faction introduced a motion asking for a preparatory study for a Jewish University. Despite something of a spat with Herzl, the idea was taken forward.[17] That there was no permanent rift between the two men was demonstrated the following year when Herzl asked Weizmann to draw up a plan for a Jewish University.[18]

Although the idea proved premature, Weizmann continued to nurse it, and it led to an important meeting. After visiting his family in Pinsk for Passover in 1903, he made his way to Warsaw to meet Nahum Sokolow, who chaired a local committee on behalf of the proposed university.[19] It was the beginning of a remarkable partnership. Born in Russian Poland in 1861, Sokolow was a writer of distinction in both Hebrew and Polish. Moving to London in 1914, he was to become an indispensable aide to Weizmann in the critical negotiations of the First World War, and joined him in presenting the Zionist case in Paris in 1919.

Even more important during this period was Weizmann's growing attachment to an attractive young Russian medical student, Vera Chatzmann, whom he met at the Jewish Club in Geneva in November 1900. Vera's father, originally from Vilnius, had served in the Imperial Army, which allowed him to live at Rostov-on-Don, outside the Pale, where he raised his family. Although he was eight years her senior, Weizmann and Vera shared a love of music, and they began to meet for tea in the Café Landolt in Geneva. But Weizmann was still making his way in the academic world and increasingly involved in the world of Zionism, while Vera had her medical degree to complete. There was also the inconvenient fact that he was already engaged to someone else. Nevertheless, by the summer of 1901 he was writing to Vera in terms which showed the depth of his feelings for her, and his engagement to Sophia Getzova was broken off. Sophia never married, but by a curious byway of fate became Professor of Pathological Anatomy at Hebrew University in Jerusalem which Weizmann did so much to found.[20]

As their romance developed, Weizmann became caught up in Zionism's first major crisis, provoked by a new outbreak of pogroms in the Tsarist empire, normally associated with the activities of the monarchist societies commonly known as the Black Hundreds. What was driving Herzl was the concept of the *Judennot*, the need of the Jews to find relief, and confirmation that the dawn of a new century had not altered this need was not long in coming. In the week of Passover and Easter 1903, crowds rampaged through the city of Kishinev, now Chisinau in Moldova, killing some 50 Jews, injuring over 1,000 and destroying 1,500 houses. The Kishinev pogrom, which was but the first in a series, confirmed Herzl in his pessimistic forecast of the Jews' future. At this point his colleague Leopold Greenberg, editor of the *Jewish Chronicle*, had a fateful meeting with Joseph Chamberlain, the British Colonial Secretary, on 20 May 1903. Chamberlain told him that Kishinev had convinced him that Herzl was right to argue that the Jews needed to get out of Eastern Europe, but questioned where they could go. The Zionists had been talking of possibilities in El Arish in the Sinai Desert and of Cyprus, but Chamberlain dismissed these, suggesting instead land in East Africa, where he believed that a million people could be settled. In subsequent communications with Chamberlain, this offer was confirmed as fertile land in what would later become Kenya, though it has always been known as the 'Uganda Offer'.[21]

Herzl was well aware that East Africa was not Palestine, but was all too conscious of what was happening in the Russian empire, which he had just visited, and that the world's greatest empire was holding out the possibility of a rescue plan. It was on that basis that he presented the offer to the Sixth Zionist Congress in Basel in August 1903. The Congress voted on the somewhat tortured resolution that it appoint an advisory committee to assist a smaller committee which was to go to East Africa to investigate the possibility, but everyone knew that what was really at stake was the principle. The vote went in Herzl's favour by 295 to 178, but with 132 abstentions. What mattered was the nature and scale of the opposition, with which Weizmann was fully engaged. What was interesting about the opposition was that it was rooted in the large Russian delegation, including those from Kishinev, the very people whose fate Herzl sought to ease.

Weizmann, still a delegate from Pinsk, denounced the Uganda scheme at a meeting of the Russian delegation, concluding with the peroration that the British would make them a better offer.[22] It was an sulphurous affair, in which Weizmann's father and brother supported Herzl, and it was to get still worse. Ussishkin, who had been absent in Palestine at the time of the Congress, launched a bitter attack on the Uganda project when he returned to Russia. Then the Russian leaders, the *Neinsager* or 'Nay-sayers' as they were known, met at Kharkov to pass a resolution denouncing Herzl for violating the original Basel Programme of 1897, which had committed the movement to Palestine. With his movement in disarray, Herzl laboured throughout the winter of 1903/4 to effect some kind of reconciliation, but for some time he had been suffering from heart problems and on 3 July 1904 he died, aged only 44.[23] The Uganda Offer did not long survive him, being rejected at the Seventh Zionist Congress in 1905. Leadership of the movement passed to David Wolfssohn, a German Jew of Lithuanian birth, whom Weizmann caustically dismissed as possessing neither personality nor vision.[24] That Zionism was now led from Berlin was to become a matter of some consequence a decade later, though that could not have been foreseen at the time.

Even less predictable were the consequences of the move

Weizmann undertook in 1904 to the University of Manchester in the north of England. The circumstances are not altogether clear, but he saw no future in Geneva, and he had a good doctorate, backed up by a number of patents and research papers. Despite his opposition to it, the Uganda offer had shown that British politicians were responsive to Zionism, and he had a letter of introduction to Professor William Henry Perkin of Manchester University, whose chemistry department he knew had a good reputation. Perkin was willing to rent him a laboratory, and from this somewhat unpromising beginning Weizmann set about learning English and gaining a foothold in the university. It says something for his determination that by January 1905 he was ready to give his first chemistry lecture in English, and in July he was appointed assistant in the chemistry department.[25] When Vera completed her medical degree in Switzerland the following year, the way was open for them to marry. The ceremony took place at Zoppot near Danzig in August 1906, and the newly-weds made their way to Manchester. Although she took pains to disguise it from her husband, Vera initially disliked the city, not least for its climate. She had to learn English and her Swiss degree did not entitle her to practise medicine until she had undertaken further classes in Manchester, which she did from 1911 to 1913, graduating with a medal. To achieve this in a language she had only just acquired speaks for itself.[26] With Weizmann often absent on Zionist business, and money sometimes scarce, it was a hard enough start to the marriage, but it survived, and Vera subsequently went on to her own distinguished medical career.[27] Their first son, Benjamin, was born in 1907, followed by Michael in 1916.

Manchester was a far cry from the hurly-burly of continental Zionist politics, but neither was it a backwater. A highly political city, the Conservative Member of Parliament for its Eastern Division since 1885 had been Arthur James Balfour. A lifelong bachelor, communicant in both the Presbyterian Church of Scotland and the Anglican Church of England, he had an interest in philosophy beyond what was normally expected of politicians, publishing respected books on the subject. His languid manner concealed a man of steel. From 1887 to 1891, he held the demanding post of Chief Secretary for Ireland where his handling of the country's affairs at a particularly turbulent time earned him the title 'Bloody Balfour', and forced him to carry a pistol for several years. Becoming Prime Minister in 1902, he presided over an administration which tore itself apart on the issue of tariff reform. At the end of 1905, he resigned in favour of the Liberals, provoking a general election. It was, of course, his Colonial Secretary who had raised the prospect of the 'Uganda Offer', and Balfour

Arthur James Balfour, First Earl of Balfour (1848–1930), was the author of the Balfour Declaration. A Scot, he was a distinguished philosopher as well as a Conservative statesman. Making his name as Chief Secretary for Ireland, he was Prime Minister from 1902–5. During the First World War, he was First Lord of the Admiralty from 1915–16, and then Foreign Secretary from 1916 to 1919. Weizmann first met him in 1906, and the two men travelled to Jerusalem for the inauguration of Hebrew University in 1925.

was sufficiently interested in the matter to find out why the Zionists had turned against it. The essential link was his Conservative party chairman in Manchester, Charles Dreyfus, who was also chairman of the Manchester Zionist Society. It was Dreyfus, a keen supporter of the Uganda scheme as it happened, who recommended to Balfour that he should meet Weizmann as one of its leading opponents. It was to prove the most fateful encounter of Weizmann's life.[28]

Their meeting took place on 9 January 1906 in the Queen's

Hotel in Manchester's Piccadilly, in the midst of the general election which resulted in Balfour losing his seat. Balfour was clearly concerned to find out why the Uganda Offer had aroused such opposition, especially since he felt that it offered a practical way forward. Weizmann responded by emphasising the spiritual side of Zionism, which he maintained could only be fulfilled by Palestine, and asked if he were to offer Paris instead of London would Balfour accept it. To Balfour's reply that they already had London, Weizmann countered that the Jews had had Jerusalem when London was still a marsh. It is difficult to gauge the real impact of this meeting, particularly since Balfour made no effort to maintain the contact, but his niece and biographer Blanche Dugdale recorded how he often referred to the conversation and the impression Weizmann had made on him. Weizmann, too, was convinced of its importance for subsequent events.[29]

Balfour was a sophisticated political veteran, but Weizmann was also in contact with the young Winston Churchill, who, having defected from the Conservatives, was contesting North-West Manchester in the Liberal interest. The two men met on two occasions in the course of the election.[30] Descendant of the Duke of Marlborough, son of a leading Conservative, soldier, foreign correspondent and author, as Colonial Secretary in 1921-2 Churchill was to become a major influence on the affairs of Palestine, while his later career belongs to history. In short, far from being an isolated outpost, Manchester was offering Weizmann openings in British politics which he could scarcely have imagined when he moved there, and which were to prove of incalculable value in the years ahead.

Manchester also provided him with his Zionist base. His opposition to Herzl and the Uganda Offer had made him *persona non grata* with Leopold Greenberg of the *Jewish Chronicle*, and he was not invited to address Zionist meetings in the capital. Instead, he used Manchester as a base to tour the scattered Jewish communities in the cities of the north of England, as well as in Glasgow and Edinburgh. These poor Jewish groups responded to him in a way in which the British Jewish elite did not. In 1909, many of the most prominent Anglo-Jewish figures, including Leopold de Rothschild, Claude Montefiore, Sir Philip Magnus, Robert Waley Cohen and Osmond d'Avigdor Goldsmid, denounced what they saw as opinions which alienated them from other Englishmen. They were supported in this by the Chief Rabbi, who issued a statement to the effect that the Jews were a religious community and not a nation. This was a portent of the opposition Weizmann was to face in 1917.[31]

In 1907, Weizmann undertook his first visit to Palestine, a climactic moment in his life which will be discussed in the following chapter. Although he never forgot his origins in the Pale, and regularly sent money home to help his younger siblings with their education, he was becoming increasingly settled in England, and his ties with Pinsk were becoming more tenuous, with the death of his father in 1911, while only in his early sixties. His scientific reputation was also growing. By 1913, he could claim an enviable list of patents and scientific papers, in such eminent publications as the *Journal of the Chemical Society*, *Biochemical Journal* and the *Proceedings of the Royal Society*.

Perkin moved to the chair of chemistry at Oxford in 1913, and Weizmann felt that the quality of his research and commitment to teaching made him an obvious candidate to succeed him. But he had recently quarrelled bitterly with Perkin, and while right was probably on Weizmann's side, this could not have happened at a worse time for him. The Manchester chair went to a rival candidate, while Weizmann had to console himself with the new title of Reader in Biochemistry. While professorships at British universities were less common than they have since become, and there was certainly no shame to his failure to get the chair, equally there is no doubt that Weizmann regarded what had happened as a major setback. An alternative did present itself in the form of an invitation to head a department in the Zionist organisation in Berlin. While in his disappointment he was tempted to accept, Vera absolutely refused to go. Neither of them liked Germany, she had just completed her medical studies, and she was now enjoying life in Manchester society. She later recorded that as a result her husband did not speak to her for three weeks. Weizmann swallowed his pride and remained in Manchester, with what fateful consequences for Zionism we now know. That he would soon rise to the summit of the movement was far from obvious, however. Wolfssohn still directed affairs from Berlin, while other, Ussishkin, Sokolow and Ha'am amongst them, were established figures, as were the distinguished authors Israel Zangwill and Max Nordau, whose writings had put them at the forefront of intellectual life, while the American Louis D Brandeis was about to come to the fore in that vibrant Jewish community.[32]

2

Palestine under the Ottomans

The Palestine which Weizmann visited for the first time in 1907 was not a country in any sense of the term, and was very different to anywhere he had so far experienced, well travelled as he was. From the early 16th century, the area had been part of the Ottoman Empire, ruled from Constantinople. It was during the reign of one of the greatest of these sultans, Suleiman the Magnificent, that Jerusalem acquired something of its modern appearance, with the construction between 1537 and 1541 of the walls around the Old City, which stand, almost intact, down to the present. Although the word 'Palestine' was widely understood to refer to the area, it was not even a single provincial entity under the empire, with the northern part lying under the Vilayet, or administrative district, of Beirut and the southern region constituting the Sanjak of Jerusalem, while across the river Jordan spread the Vilayet of Syria. Although the Empire had suffered steady retreat in Europe from the time the Habsburgs had thwarted its bid to take Vienna in 1683, and it now lagged far behind the major powers in economic and military strength, the Turks had no intention of surrendering control of their

The Ottoman Empire 1914

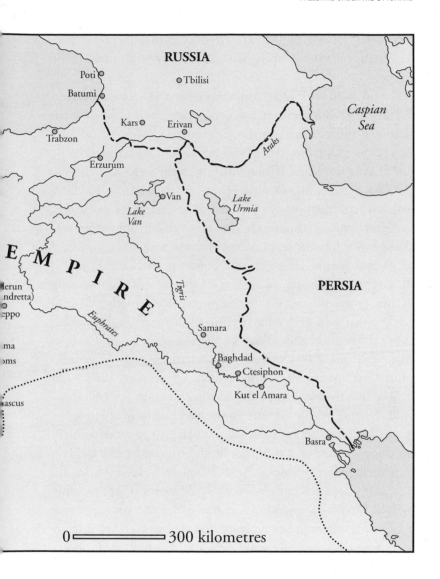

0 ⟺ 300 kilometres

territories in the Middle East, whether to an embryonic Arab nationalism or the Zionist newcomers Weizmann had come to see.

The voyage took him from Marseilles, via Alexandria, to Beirut, where he spent an uncomfortable period in quarantine, and then, at last, to the shores of Palestine at Jaffa. It was his introduction to the land which had been the focus of his dreams for years. If his autobiography is to be believed, the experience was not altogether positive. He particularly disliked Jerusalem, whose Jewish life he castigated as lacking in dignity and existing on charity. His attitude did not greatly change over time, it seems, though he did note the potential of Mount Scopus for erecting a building which could reflect the city's Jewish legacy. What, of course, he was encountering in the city was the community of pious, often elderly and generally poor Jews who were supported through the *Hallukah*, charitable collections taken in the synagogues of Europe. Although this was a system which had existed for generations, Weizmann, the modern man of science, could not believe that they had anything to offer a future Jewish homeland. Neither was he greatly impressed by many of the more recent Jewish colonies, since they, too, he felt, were dependent on charity, albeit of a different kind. Nor did he like the fact that they were employing Arab labourers. However, he did note with approval a number of settlements where recently arrived Russian Jews, who had come into the country from 1904, were offering better hope for the future through the enterprise they were showing, not least through their ability to compete with Arab labour.[1]

In viewing these communities, Weizmann was encountering the reality of the somewhat haphazard nature of Jewish settlement since the 1880s. In fact, Palestine was predominantly Arab, and the Zionist enterprise to which he was so deeply committed could only be measured against that reality, of which he was well aware.[2] Though long dismissed as the 'sick man of Europe', there was more to the Ottoman Empire than met the eye. By the time of Weizmann's visit to Palestine, the Turks had been expelled from most of Europe and were to lose even more in the First Balkan War of 1912–13, but this made them all the more determined to hold on to their extensive territories in the Middle East. While these lands were overwhelmingly Sunni Arab in composition, there were important exceptions, and the empire was, in fact, a fascinating mosaic. Shi'a Arabs had important areas of strength in what were to become Iraq and Lebanon. Communities of Alawites and Druses existed along the eastern Mediterranean. The principal non-Arab groups were the Muslim Kurds and the Christian Armenians. There were also flourishing Christian minorities in many other areas, perhaps the most notable of which were the Maronites of modern-day Lebanon, who enjoyed a close relationship with the French and the Vatican. Outside the Holy Land there were sizeable Jewish communities, not least that of Baghdad where Jews had lived since the time of the Babylonian captivity. The distinctive nature of the Christian and Jewish minorities was recognised by the Turks through the *millet* system which allowed them a degree of self-regulation based upon their religious laws. Having said that, what bound the predominantly Muslim Arab territories to their Turkish rulers was religion. The empire was the last remaining bastion of Islamic political power in a world dominated by the expanding Christian empires of Europe, and the Ottoman Sultan was also the Caliph, the spiritual successor to the Prophet. The Young Turk revolution of 1908, which brought to power the Committee of Union and Progress, promised a revitalisation of the empire, even though the revolutionaries went on to assert its Turkish, as opposed to Islamic, nature. The empire was also drawing close to Germany, the most vibrant power in continental Europe. Despite the setbacks in the Balkans, and in Libya at the hands of the Italians in 1911, the Turkish armies were tough and capably led, as the British imperial forces were to find out to their cost in the debacles at Gallipoli in 1915 and Kut in 1916. In short, the Ottoman Empire neither seemed on the verge of collapse nor in any mood to surrender control of the Holy Land to the Zionists or anyone else.

If the situation seemed to hold scant promise for the Zionists, it was hardly any better for Palestine's Arab majority. The Palestinians reflected the broader Arab society of the empire in that there were identifiable Christian communities, especially in cities like Bethlehem and Nazareth, which had associations with the life of Christ, but the overwhelming majority were Sunni Muslims. Palestinian Arab society was predominantly agricultural. While there was some industry, for example the soap trade of Nablus, most urban economic activity, such as handicrafts, weaving and construction, was related in some way to the agricultural sector. The main inhibiting factor for Palestinian agriculture was, as it has remained, the availability of water for irrigation, or rather the comparative lack of it. The country's principal river, the Jordan, was unsuitable for irrigation purposes, and hence the peasant cultivators of Palestine had to be careful that their farming methods and crops were adapted to this and did not cause the erosion of what fertile soil they had. The winter crops were wheat and barley, while in the summer sesame and durra were harvested. Palestinian figs and olives were well known, and sheep and goats provided the livestock, well adapted to the hilly terrain of the country's interior.[3] The cultivators were the *fellahin*, who constituted the backbone of the Palestinian population. Passionately attached to the soil they farmed, their title to it was often insecure, at least by European standards. The land of Palestine was held under various systems, decided according to the Turkish land law of 1858. Much of it was designated as state, or *miri*, land, which was then allotted to peasant cultivators, subject to continuous cultivation. Under the *Musha'a* system, land was rotated, which at least ensured that everyone would have a share of the better land, but did not encourage soil improvement or fertilisation.[4] A further significant element of the Palestinian population were the Bedouin, who led a nomadic way of life, chiefly in the Negev desert in the south but also in Galilee.

While village leaders were important in their locality, power and status in Palestinian society rested primarily with the urban elites, who were also extensive landowners. Like other imperial rulers, the Turks helped sustain their empire through the co-option and co-operation of such groups, who were known as the *a'yan* or 'notables'. The leading *a'yan* families, the Husaynis, Nashashibis, Khalidis, Jarallas and Nusseibehs, were to provide the leadership of Arab Palestine for the period under review. The Husaynis enjoyed particular prestige since they had provided the city's mayor and for a long period the religious office of Mufti of Jerusalem had generally been held by a member of the family.[5]

The origins and development of Arab nationalism in the late 19th and early 20th centuries remain obscure, although it was hardly surprising that some intellectuals caught the winds of national identity which were blowing so strongly in contemporary Europe. If anything, these feelings intensified once the Young Turks pursued their policies of Turkification after 1908. The Arabs possessed, after all, legacies of a past when their own empire stood at the peak of world civilisation. Even so, if there was a prevailing view amongst Arab nationalists it was for increased autonomy within the empire rather than for full independence. This was still a fledgling movement, with its centres in Damascus and Beirut.[6] There was, in fact, little indication in the early 20th century that the Ottoman Empire in the Middle East was about to shatter into Turkish and Arab components, although there were sentiments amongst the latter which the British were able to tap into, and exploit, after 1914.

For Jews, Christians and Muslims alike, Jerusalem was the heart of the Holy Land, even if Weizmann did not greatly take to it at first sight. While it is easy to see those aspects of it which he disliked, the city was, and still is, a place of infinite fascination. The Old City, enclosed by its Turkish walls, contained sites sacred to the three great monotheistic religions, Judaism, Christianity and Islam. At its south-east corner was the area known to the Jews as the Temple Mount on Mount Moriah, where the First and Second Temples had stood before the latter was destroyed by the Romans in the course of the Jewish revolts. All that survived the Roman pillage was the western retaining wall of the Second Temple built by King Herod, and it was this fragment which had become the focus of Jewish longing and religious devotion throughout succeeding centuries. As Jews gathered there to lament what had happened, it became known as the Wailing Wall. At the time of Weizmann's visit to the city, it was approached by a narrow and unprepossessing lane, but its significance for the Jews was profound, nonetheless.

Jerusalem also contained the sites associated with the death of Christ. Across the Kidron Valley from the Old City lay the Garden of Gethsemane at the foot of the Mount of Olives. Within the Old City were traced the 14 Stations of the Cross which culminated within the Church of the Holy Sepulchre, where most Christian denominations believed that the crucifixion, burial and resurrection of Jesus had taken place. Although these associations gave the city a unique status amongst the world's Christians, Christianity was a minority faith amongst the Palestinians and if we are to understand why Jerusalem became a particular focus of Arab-Jewish tensions then it is to Islam that we must turn. What to Jews was the Temple Mount, for Muslims was the *Haram al-Sherif*, the 'Noble Sanctuary', from which Muhammad made his journey to heaven. On a platform of stunning beauty there were, and are, two of the finest mosques in the Islamic world. The Dome of the Rock housed the Rock of Moriah, where it was believed Abraham was prepared to sacrifice his son, Isaac, while the neighbouring Mosque of Al Aqsa, was third in importance only to the mosques of Mecca and Medina. Since this was also the area where King Solomon's Temple stood, with its Holy of Holies, then its unique place in religious history may be easily understood. Hence, the term Holy Land was not lightly borne. In addition to Jerusalem, Safed, Tiberias and Hebron were holy cities to the Jews. Like Jerusalem, Hebron illustrated both the close links between Judaism and Islam and the potential for conflict between them. In Jewish tradition, it was the resting place of Adam and Eve. It also was the location of the Tombs of the Patriarchs, Abraham, Isaac and Jacob, with their wives Sarah, Rebecca and Leah. What to Jews was the Tomb of the Patriarchs was for Muslims the Mosque of Ibrahim. Hebron was to bring into sharp focus the conflict between Arab and Jew, though that lay in the future.

Modern Jewish settlement was a rather different story, however, and it was this which interested Weizmann, not always favourably as we have seen. The origins of such settlement was *Hibbat Zion* , the 'Love of Zion', the movement which had aroused such passion in his boyhood imagination over 20 years earlier. In 1882, a small group of the *Hovevei Zion* made its way to Palestine, where their first settlements were Rishon le-Zion, Rosh Pinnah and Petah Tikvah, followed by others such as Rehovoth (which was to become Weizmann's home from 1934), Hadera and Metulla. They were not an immediate success, for the simple reasons that they were inadequately funded and that the settlers were inexperienced farmers. It was an inauspicious beginning for modern Jewish settlement in Palestine, which might have fallen at the first hurdle had it not been for the intervention of Baron Edmond de Rothschild, philanthropist and scion of the great French banking and winemaking dynasty. As the little settlements started to founder, Rothschild was persuaded to help, providing considerable financial backing, albeit at the cost of close supervision by his agents. With their assistance, a wine industry was created, followed by citrus production, which succeeded in stimulating an economic base for the settlements. In the course of this endeavour, two things were happening which Weizmann was to castigate in the course of his 1907 visit. The first was their employment of Arab labour, but probably more worrying from his perspective was the extent of their dependence on Rothschild's beneficence, which seemed too close to the *Hallukah* system he so disliked in Jerusalem.[7] Relations between Weizmann and Rothschild were never warm, it seems.

These men and women constituted the First *Aliya*, the first immigration or 'going up' to the Holy Land. Their successors of the Second *Aliya*, which began in 1904, were much more to Weizmann's taste, and in the course of his 1907 visit he had liked what he had seen. What impelled them was the backwash of the failed Russian revolution of 1904–5 and the renewed spate of pogroms which broke out in its wake. What marked them out from their immediate predecessors were their socialist convictions allied to a belief that the Jews needed to work for themselves as part of their national development. One such immigrant was the 19-year-old David Gryn from Plonsk in the Polish part of the Russian empire, who changed his name to Ben-Gurion, a leader who had perished in the Jewish Revolt against the Romans. His fortunes were to become intertwined with those of Weizmann, becoming pivotal to the development of Zionism and subsequently to the State of Israel. Their passionate commitment to Zionism apart, the two men could not have been less alike. Whereas Weizmann was tall, urbane and familiar with the educational systems of Russia, Germany, Switzerland and Great Britain, Ben-Gurion was short and feisty, his higher education confined to a brief spell studying law in Istanbul, which was cut short by the outbreak of war. Perhaps the clue to Ben-Gurion's attitude to the older man was his observation in old age that compared with draining the swamps of Galilee the lobbying of the well-dressed Zionists in Western Europe was futile.[8]

David Ben-Gurion (1886–1973) was born in what is now Poland, and migrated to Palestine in 1906. In the 1920s, he became prominent in the *Histadrut* trade union movement and was an uneasy ally of Weizmann. On 14 May 1948, he proclaimed the State of Israel in Tel-Aviv, becoming Prime Minister until 1953, and then again from 1955 to 1963, thus presiding over the country's fortunes during the wars of 1948–9 and 1956. He was instrumental in ensuring that Weizmann's presidency was purely a ceremonial one. Israel's international airport is named after him.

The young immigrant's change of surname was emblematic of a historic initiative of the Second *Aliya*; namely, the adoption and fostering of the Hebrew language. Most arrivals at that time would have spoken Yiddish, and would almost certainly also have known Russian or possibly Polish. German, of course, was the language of choice for the cultivated Central European Jewish middle class, like Herzl himself. Hebrew was the sacred language of the scriptures and worship in the synagogue, revered as such. But revival of language was an integral part of the story of national reawakening in Europe, and Zionism proved to be no different. The driving force behind this development was Eliezer Ben Yehuda, originally Perlman, who settled in Palestine in 1882, and who preached, and practised, the exclusive use of Hebrew. Ben Yehuda clearly recognised the need to bring this ancient language into the modern age if it were to have any future, and this was embodied in the Hebrew Thesaurus he published in 1910. His lead was enthusiastically taken up by the new immigrants, although regarded with suspicion and disfavour by many orthodox Jews for whom Hebrew was a sacred language not to be used for mundane matters.

Foundations were also being laid in other ways. In 1908, Dr Arthur Ruppin set up the Palestine Office in Jaffa, the purpose of which was to bring some impetus and organisation to land purchase. The following year, in the apparently unpromising sand dunes to the north of the ancient Arab port of Jaffa, a start was made to a new suburb which in time was to grow into a thriving Jewish metropolis. This was called Tel Aviv, 'the hill of the spring'. By 1914 it had attracted around 2,000 inhabitants. The driving force behind it came from the Russian Jewish immigrant Meir Dizengoff, who became chairman of the Town Council in 1910, and whose name was to become synonymous with the city's development for almost three decades. Although it was to suffer a serious setback during the war, under Dizengoff's direction Tel Aviv expanded dramatically in the 1920s and 1930s, in time overshadowing Jaffa.[9] Elsewhere, Jews were settling in Haifa and new suburbs were springing up in Jerusalem. In short, however modestly, Zionism was establishing the basis for subsequent urbanisation.

These years just prior to the outbreak of war saw the Zionists put in hand two other enterprises which were to serve them well in the future. The first, education, lay close to Weizmann's heart. Although he was not the first to advocate the creation of a Jewish university, there is no question but that he supplied its early dynamic. First proposed at the Fifth Zionist Congress in 1901 by Weizmann's Democratic Faction, the following year a pamphlet, *Eine Jüdische Hochschule*, appeared over his name, together with Dr Martin Buber of Vienna and Dr Berthold Feivel of Geneva. The concept then languished for a time, but at the Eleventh Zionist Congress in Vienna in 1913, Weizmann read a paper on the subject of establishing a Hebrew University, as a result of which he was asked to organise a University Committee. His speech emphasised that in creating a university, the Zionist movement would be building for the future. His colleague in Palestine, Arthur Ruppin, was to find a suitable site. This was acquired in 1914 on Jerusalem's Mount Scopus, which Weizmann had noted with favour in 1907, though the establishment of the university was to be delayed because of the war. With singularly unfortunate timing, Weizmann's group met in Berlin on 18 July 1914, and their deliberations were to be taken forward in Paris on 10 August.[10]

A further initiative, largely inspired by German Jews, was

the foundation in Haifa in 1912 of the Technikum, destined, as its name indicates, to act as a centre for technical education. Its founders assumed that the language of instruction would be German, hardly surprisingly in view of its genesis and the pre-eminence of Germany in science and technology at that time. But Weizmann and other Zionists strongly disagreed, arguing instead for Hebrew. At a meeting of the Technikum's board in Berlin in June 1914, Weizmann was completely out-voted on the issue. The result was a strike by the staff and other Jewish teachers in Palestine. Like Hebrew University, the institution's progress was halted by the outbreak of hos-tilities, but when it opened in 1924 it was as the Technion, not the Technikum, teaching in Hebrew. As Weizmann later observed, the language controversy had a significant by-prod-uct, since during the war it enabled him to counter critics on the Allied side who pointed out that the Zionist headquarters were in Berlin.[11] The other initiative, modest in scope though it was, presented a less benign scenario. Arab attacks resulted in the creation of the *Ha-Shomer*, or 'Watchman', Society, the purpose of which was the defence of the scattered Jewish settlements. That the need for such a body existed, efficient though it appears to have been, was hardly a happy augury.

The decade prior to the outbreak of war had seen a dis-tinct acceleration in Jewish settlement in Palestine, as well as a deepening of the Zionist presence. In 1907, Weizmann saw, and approved of, the activities of the members of the new *Aliya*. Their achievements undoubtedly enabled him to present a positive account in the critical years ahead of what the Zionist movement was capable of doing. Even so, in 1914 the prospects for Zionism remained problematic. Palestine was an overwhelmingly Arab country, firmly locked into an Ottoman Empire ruled by a group of men who were

·determined to revive its fortunes. As with so many things, the assassination of Archduke Franz Ferdinand, heir to the thrones of Austria and Hungary, and his wife by a Serb nationalist in Sarajevo on 28 June 1914 set in train a chain of events which were to transform the fortunes of Arab, Jew and Turk alike; however unlikely that might have seemed at the time.

3

War and the Balfour Declaration

What the future of Zionism, and of Palestine, might have been if the world had not gone to war in 1914 no one can now tell, but since it soon became clear that this was a struggle on an epic scale, the powers were forced to speculate on what a peace settlement might look like. In considering the historic nature of Weizmann's achievement in the years that followed, it is necessary to appreciate two things. First, political Zionism had been the product of Central Europe, and its headquarters were in Berlin. More importantly, its numerical strength lay in the Jewish communities of the Tsarist empire – their oppressor but Britain's ally – by whom the armies of Germany and Austria-Hungary were understandably seen as liberators. There was nothing pre-ordained about the alliance between Zionism and the British Empire which Weizmann was instrumental in forging.[1]

It was not inevitable that the Ottoman Empire would enter the war on the side of the Central Powers, but in November 1914 the rulers of Turkey did link their fate with that of Berlin and Vienna. Despite the fact that Turkish military forces were less technologically advanced than those of the other powers,

Germany and Austria-Hungary had gained a major asset. The Turks threatened Britain at two key points in the Middle East. The first was the Suez Canal through which Britain was drawing troops and supplies from India, Australia and New Zealand. The other was the Persian Gulf, the source of oil for the fast battleships of the *Queen Elizabeth* class, the cutting edge of the Royal Navy. Just as dangerous was Turkey's appeal in the Islamic world, since France recruited widely in her North African territories, while the Indian Army, the British Empire's sole trained reserve, drew heavily on the Muslim community in the north-west of the sub-continent. Finally, Turkey had a long frontier with Russia, whose armies were hard-pressed enough at the hands of the Germans and Austrians. There was never any doubt that war with Turkey would have to take second place to the main fronts in Europe, but neither could it be ignored in Petrograd, Paris, and especially London.

This was evident almost from the start. On 9 November 1914, the British Prime Minister Herbert Asquith made a speech in London's Guildhall in which he raised the future of the Ottoman Empire. The possible fate of Palestine also excited the interest of the distinguished Liberal Herbert Samuel (1870–1963), Member of Parliament for Cleveland. A first class graduate of Oxford University, Samuel had already made his mark in British history by becoming the first Jew to sit in the Cabinet, if we discount the Anglican Benjamin Disraeli. A representative of the assimilated Jewish elite which Weizmann instinctively distrusted, Samuel, by his own admission, had taken no real part in Zionism until the war with Turkey gave him cause to think about it.[2] On the same day that Asquith delivered his Guildhall speech, Samuel visited his Cabinet colleague the Foreign Secretary Sir Edward Grey, arguing that in the event of a Turkish defeat they should think about the possibility of a Jewish state in Palestine.[3]

Meanwhile, Weizmann, who had made a difficult journey back from an attempted family holiday in Switzerland, was also alive to the new possibilities, and here, too, the Manchester connection proved to be invaluable to him. Shortly after his return to the city he met over dinner C P Scott, the editor for over four decades of the leading Liberal newspaper the *Manchester Guardian*, a man with ready access to the highest reaches of the party. Evidently intrigued by his new acquaintance, Scott invited Weizmann to his house to discuss Jewish affairs. After Weizmann had confided in him his hatred of the Russian Empire, which was candid of him given that the two countries were fighting on the same side, and of the Jewish hopes for Palestine, Scott pointed out that there was now a Jew in the Cabinet, and that he would like to put him in touch with the Chancellor of the Exchequer, David Lloyd George.

Charles Prestwich Scott (1846–1932) was editor of the *Manchester Guardian* from 1872 to 1929. A graduate in Classics from the University of Oxford, and Member of Parliament for Leigh in Lancashire from 1895 to 1906, he was one of the most influential figures in the Liberal Party. He met Weizmann in 1914, and was instrumental in arranging his initial meetings with Samuel and Lloyd George. A supporter of Zionism, he remained an invaluable conduit between Weizmann and leading Liberal politicians.

Seizing the opportunity, Weizmann followed up the meeting in a letter to Scott on 12 November, in which he argued that if Britain could encourage Jewish emigration to Palestine as a British dependency, then they could develop it and help safeguard the Suez Canal. This was precisely the line of argument which he was to refine over the next few years, and which would form the basis of the case he eventually placed before the Peace Conference. Equally, there is no doubt that Weizmann instantly grasped the implications of Asquith's Guildhall speech, since on the same day of his letter to Scott he also wrote to Ahad Ha'am in quite excited terms, saying that the speech should prompt them into action, and that in the event of victory Britain would be in control of Palestine.[4]

Scott proved to be as good as his word. At a breakfast meeting with Lloyd George on 27 November, he raised the future of Palestine. Lloyd George seemed interested in the idea of some kind of partly Jewish state, and revealed that Samuel had already discussed this with him. He responded positively to Scott's idea of a meeting with Weizmann, suggesting that this should also include Samuel.[5] This could not take place for a couple of months, but Scott had opened up a crucial contact, since Lloyd George was destined to be in a position to shape the course of events. While that lay in the future, Lloyd George was already one of the leading, not to say contentious, figures in British political life. Born in Manchester in 1863 of Welsh origin, he had been Chancellor since 1908, had played a significant part in the search for an Irish settlement between 1912 and 1914, and was to go on to hold the key offices of Minister of Munitions in 1915–16 and Minister of War in 1916. Then, in December that year, he replaced Asquith to lead Britain to victory in the war, and to play a central role in the subsequent Peace Conference.

In the meantime, Weizmann had his first meeting with Samuel on 10 December. Samuel revealed that he had been quietly watching Zionism for some time, and that with Turkey in the war the realisation of its aims was possible. He wanted Weizmann to keep in contact.[6] The promised meeting with Lloyd George took place over breakfast on 15 January 1915. The account Weizmann gave in his autobiography, which places the meeting in early December 1914, says that

Samuel, Scott and the Labour MP Josiah Wedgwood were also present. In general, Lloyd George seemed well disposed to what he heard from Weizmann, advising him that he could expect opposition from the assimilation-supporting Jewish community, and especially from the rising Liberal politician Edwin Montagu, who was, as it happened, Samuel's cousin. Weizmann also recollected that Samuel revealed the fact that he was preparing a memorandum which he was going to give to the Prime Minister.[7]

Although Samuel never actually joined the Zionist organisation, he pressed ahead with his memorandum, which he first circulated to colleagues in January 1915, followed by a revised version in March. What he argued was that, lying as it did so close to the vital artery of the Suez Canal, Palestine should not be allowed to fall under the control of a major European power such as France or Germany. Instead, he suggested that it should become a British protectorate. On the question of Zionism, he admitted that the time was not ripe for the creation of a Jewish state in Palestine, but that under a British protectorate regulated Jewish immigration could lead in time to a Jewish majority which could be granted some form of self-government. It does not seem that Samuel's document excited any great degree of interest amongst his colleagues. Asquith, in particular, was totally dismissive, but just the same the idea of a future British administration in Palestine which could encourage Jewish aspirations had entered into political discourse at the highest level. Its time had not yet come, but it would, and Samuel made sure that Weizmann and Scott were aware of feelings in the Cabinet.[8]

What he learned from Samuel of the Cabinet's feelings prompted Weizmann to gather his thoughts together in a long letter to Scott on 23 March. He now believed that there was a feeling in the Cabinet which was sympathetic to the realisation of Zionist aspirations in Palestine, and to proposing them at a peace conference, but that there was a reluctance to make the country a British responsibility. What he was referring to was a section of Liberal opinion which was opposed to a policy of annexation. On the other hand, there was the belief that Palestine should not come under another major power. That led him to the conclusion that Palestine should be a temporary British protectorate, to the mutual advantage of Britain and the Jews. Such an arrangement, he argued, would help guard the Egyptian border, earn Britain the thanks of Jews around the world, and enable the Jews to act as a bridge between East and West. It is clear that both Weizmann and Samuel were working in the same direction. That this was the case was confirmed by Scott on 15 April when he related to Weizmann a dinner conversation with Samuel and Lloyd George in the course of which they had raised the question of Zionism. Samuel had spoken warmly about it, and Scott observed to Weizmann that Lloyd George was more important than Asquith, correctly as events were to demonstrate.[9]

In any case, the future of Palestine was little more than a matter of academic interest at that time, since the military defeat of Turkey was a long way off. In 1915, Britain suffered one of her worst military debacles in the ill-fated Gallipoli campaign, which seemed to have wrecked the political career of Churchill, who had largely inspired it. In Palestine, the Jews were naturally fearful for their position, given the fact that most of the recent settlers were from Russia, with which Turkey was now at war. The governorship of Syria and Palestine was in the hands of Ahmed Jamal Pasha, a ruthless member of the Young Turk movement, who distrusted equally Armenians, Jews and Arab nationalists, so much so that he went down in Arab memory as 'Jamal the Butcher', and was assassinated in 1922 by an Armenian. The Jews of Palestine were spared some of the worst of his attentions by the American Ambassador to Constantinople, Henry Morgenthau, and the fact that the Germans did not wish to alienate Jewish opinion. Even so, Jamal Pasha cracked down hard on Zionist activity. By the end of 1915, over 11,000 Jews, including Ben-Gurion, had been deported, mostly to Egypt. While some Jews were accepted for service in the Ottoman army, in 1917 Jamal Pasha ordered the evacuation of the new settlement of Tel Aviv. As the economy started to collapse, hunger hit the Arab and Jewish population alike.[10]

The response of young Jews who had been expelled to Egypt was to rally to the British cause, forming the Zion Mule Corps, a transport company, which served with distinction at Gallipoli in 1915. Its commanding officer was an adventurous Irish Protestant, Lieutenant-Colonel John Henry Patterson DSO, who in 1916 published his account in *With the Zionists in Gallipoli*. Patterson is perhaps best remembered for his book about Africa, *The Man-Eaters of Tsavo*, which he published in 1907 (and is, at the time of writing, still in print). So convinced was Patterson of the potential of the men he had led, that on his return to London he campaigned for the recruitment of Jewish battalions, three of which subsequently fought under his command in Palestine. Patterson, who has a reasonable claim to be regarded as one of the founders of the future Israel Defence Forces, retained an interest in Zionism for the rest of his life.[11] The Jewish driving forces behind the Mule Corps were Joseph Trumpeldor, a one-armed veteran of the Russo-Japanese war, who had become the first Jewish officer in the Tsarist army, and Vladimir, or Ze'ev, Jabotinsky.

An Odessa-born journalist, Jabotinsky had begun to make his mark as an orator at the pre-war Zionist congresses, and had already clashed with Weizmann over the proposed Hebrew University. In the 1920s he was to quarrel fundamentally with Weizmann, seceding from the Zionist organisation in 1925 to form the right-wing Revisionist Zionists. He is generally acknowledged to be the founder and intellectual dynamo behind the Zionist right, which eventually came into its inheritance in 1977 with the election victory of Menachem Begin, and which has been a powerful force in Israeli politics ever since.[12]

In April 1915, Asquith's government appointed a committee chaired by Sir Maurice de Bunsen to examine what Britain's likely interests would be in the event of a Turkish defeat, particularly since France and Russia would also be eyeing up the possibilities. While its work had no practical effect, its deliberations do indicate where British thinking on the region was going, even at this stage of the war. One possibility was of an empire reformed along federal lines, which would give national self-expression to Turks, Arabs and Armenians. The British liked federal schemes, as they had shown in Australia, and were to try them in other parts of their own empire, mostly without success. But in the event of a break-up of the empire, de Bunsen's committee recommended that Britain should acquire Mesopotamia from Basra at the head of the Persian Gulf to Mosul, her oil interests in that part of the Middle East being paramount. This would be connected to the port of Haifa. The French would have their interests recognised in the districts around Damascus and Beirut, while the Straits would go to Russia, fulfilling a long-standing ambition for access to the Aegean and Mediterranean. Palestine would require special agreement amongst the three Christian allies, Protestants, Catholics and Orthodox each having interests there. Muslim and Jewish interests were of less importance, it seems.[13]

Other events were coming to a head in the course of 1915, which would have a significant impact on the course of the war in the Middle East, but also for future claims and counter-claims to Palestine. The British were naturally interested in acquiring allies in the region, especially someone who could act as a religious counterweight to the Sultan of Turkey, and they had found just such a man. They knew that in the Arabian peninsula, Hussein, head of the Hashemite family, was a restive subject of Constantinople. Not only was he a descendant of the Prophet Muhammad, but he was Sherif, or Guardian, of Mecca and Medina, the sites of the Holy Places of Islam. In other words, he was the perfect potential ally. As early as February 1914, his son Abdullah had visited Egypt to see how the British would regard an Arab revolt led by Hussein, so that the High Commissioner in Cairo, Sir Henry McMahon, was well aware of where he could enlist a key ally.

The resulting correspondence between McMahon and Hussein led to an Arab army loyal to the Hashemites entering the war against the Turks, but it is the nature of the promises made by the British which were to cause such controversy. The key British pledge came in a letter from McMahon to Hussein on 24 October 1915, which became so critical to the future course of relations with the Arabs, and to the debate over Palestine, that the key passage must be quoted: 'The two districts of Mersina and Alexandretta and portions of Syria lying to the west of the districts of Damascus, Homs, Hama and Aleppo cannot be said to be purely Arab and should be excluded from the limits demanded. With the above modifications, and without prejudice to our existing treaties with

Arab chiefs, we accept these limits ... Subject to the modifications, Great Britain is prepared to recognise and support the independence of the Arabs in all regions within the limits demanded by the Sherif of Mecca.' [14]

What did McMahon mean, and what were the implications of what he said? Support for the independence of the Arabs seems plain enough, and was taken at face value. When, therefore, the post-war system of Mandates was put in place it was seen by the Arabs as reneging on an obligation, and treated as such. Promises, in Arab society, are meant to be kept, and are. As for Palestine, on 12 March 1922, McMahon wrote to the Colonial Office, pleading that it had been his intention to exclude Palestine from his pledges to Hussein. He argued, somewhat limply, that the reason why he stopped with Damascus was that he could not think of anywhere further south that he could use for purposes of definition. A year later, Sir Gilbert Clayton, who had helped draft McMahon's letters, assured Samuel, by then High Commissioner in Palestine, that there had been no intention of including Palestine. On 23 July 1937, McMahon confirmed publicly in a letter to *The Times* that he had not intended to include Palestine in the area which was to be the independent Arab kingdom. [15] While these letters must be treated with some respect, it must be remembered that McMahon and Clayton were writing at a time when the future of Palestine had become a matter of acute concern, which it had not been in 1915.

It has been argued that if 'district' is taken as synonymous

> ' ... portions of Syria lying to the west of the districts of Damascus, Homs, Hama and Aleppo cannot be said to be purely Arab, and should be excluded from the limits demanded.'
>
> SIR HENRY MCMAHON TO HUSSEIN, 24 OCTOBER 1915

with Vilayet, then Palestine was excluded, since it lay to the west of the Vilayet of Syria. But this hardly stands up against the fact that there were no Vilayets of Homs or Hama, while there was a Vilayet of Aleppo, which included Alexandretta. If McMahon could not think of anywhere south of Damascus, places such as Dara'a, a rail junction with a line leading to Haifa, Amman and Aqaba, could have been identified. Crucially, of course, neither Palestine nor Jerusalem was mentioned. It is hard to escape the conclusion that by identifying districts to the west of the four cities of Damascus, Homs, Hama and Aleppo, McMahon was looking to the future of the Christian, and possibly Druse, communities of what was to become Lebanon, where Britain's ally France had long-standing interests.[16] Whether or not Palestine was part of the area pledged to Hussein has been, and doubtless will continue to be, endlessly debated, but the essential point was that the Arabs believed it to be part of their inheritance from the British.

It was in the knowledge of these negotiations, but unknown to Hussein, that Britain entered into an agreement with France in 1916, essentially dividing the Middle East between them. The Sykes-Picot Agreement, called after its authors, Sir Mark Sykes and François Georges Picot, reflected many of the ideas of the de Bunsen Committee. France was to get the stretch of the Mediterranean coast north of the port of Acre, while Britain's area was to be oil-rich Mesopotamia together with an enclave around Haifa. Other Arab areas were to become British or French protectorates. What this implied for the pledge of Arab independence hardly needs stating, but what was also significant was the emergence of an entity called 'Palestine', the boundaries of which were close to what later became the British Mandate, though without the

Negev Desert in the south. Palestine was to be international, since Britain was conscious of Catholic and Orthodox concerns over the Christian Holy Places, but also wished to keep the French at a distance from the Suez Canal. Cutting as it did across any sense of a united independent Arab kingdom, the Sykes-Picot Agreement was to be excoriated by the Arabs once its terms were revealed in the aftermath of the Bolshevik revolution in Russia.[17]

The Arab Revolt began on 5 June 1916, provoked in part by a wave of public executions of suspected Arab nationalists in Damascus and Beirut ordered by Jamal Pasha. Proclaiming Arab independence in the name of Hussein, forces led by his son Feisal defeated the isolated Turkish garrisons in the Arabian Peninsula. Then, on 6 July 1917, they captured Aqaba, opening the way for an attack northward in support of the British troops which were about to advance into Palestine under their new and vigorous commander, General Sir Edmund Allenby. Associated with Feisal was Colonel T E Lawrence, archaeologist and intelligence officer, whose exploits, as 'Lawrence of Arabia', were to become legendary.

Notwithstanding these events, which were to change the political map of the Middle East, the main British front was

King Feisal I of Iraq (1883–1933) was the son of Hussein, Sherif of Mecca, and a descendant of the Prophet Muhammad, who in 1916 brought an Arab army into the war on the British side. He met Weizmann twice in 1918, the first time in the Middle East, and then later in London. The two men established a rapport, and in the agreement of 3 January 1919 he expressed support for Jewish aspirations, though subject to a *caveat* which the Allies did not fulfil. Proclaimed King of Syria in 1920, he was soon expelled by the French. With British support, he became King of Iraq in 1921, and then worked for his new country's full independence. In retrospect, it is clear that Weizmann banked too much on his influence with the Palestinian Arabs, who were turning to their own leaders.

in France and Flanders, where the war had taken on almost unimaginable dimensions with the small British Expeditionary Force, the famous 'Old Contemptibles' of 1914, transformed into the first mass army in British history. But that brought problems, not least in the area of munitions where supply failed to match the needs of the army. This was particularly true of the artillery, and by the spring of 1915 what became known as 'The Great Shell Scandal' rocked British politics, playing no small part in the formation of a new coalition government in May. As a result, a new Ministry of Munitions was created, under the direction of David Lloyd George, charged with ensuring that the army received the supplies it needed.[18]

A particularly pressing need was for a plentiful supply of acetone, an essential ingredient in cordite, the propellant for shells and bullets, and a substance on which, as it happened, Weizmann had worked in the course of his researches into fermentation. His findings attracted the attention of the research scientists at the large Nobel munitions works at Ardeer near Irvine in Ayrshire, but a major explosion at the factory in 1915 proved to be a setback. Weizmann had already been approached by the Admiralty through Sir Frederick Nathan, who had particular responsibility for cordite, and this approach was confirmed, it seems, at a meeting with the First Lord, Winston Churchill. While the records relating to the key meetings are somewhat elliptical, Weizmann apparently met Lloyd George through Scott's good offices in June 1915, and from then on he had the green light to work on the mass production of acetone from maize. Working for the government meant that he had to take leave of absence from Manchester University and move to London. There is no question but that his work contributed significantly to the British war effort. Moreover, it gave him a new-found financial security, and it was to be the road which took him from provincial obscurity in Manchester to the hub of British politics.[19]

It was no less a person than Lloyd George who gave currency to the link between Weizmann's work on acetone and the subsequent Balfour Declaration on Zionism. According to his account, he asked Weizmann what honour he would like to be recommended for in recognition of his work. Weizmann's reply was that he wanted nothing for himself, but something could be done for his people who had aspirations of returning to their ancient homeland. Lloyd George's claim that this was the origin of the Balfour Declaration need not be taken at face value, since the dynamics were much more complex than that, but he returned to it in November 1944 when writing a foreword to a volume honouring Weizmann on his 70th birthday.[20] The rather more prosaic truth was that by 1916 Weizmann had rendered a significant service to the British state and was now a respected figure in the eyes of those at the heart of government. This assumed even greater significance after December 1916, when Lloyd George succeeded Asquith, whose interest in Zionism had never been great, as Prime Minister with none other than Balfour as his Foreign Secretary. But since Samuel had followed Asquith into political exile, an influential ally had also been lost.

Lloyd George's coalition brought into the War Cabinet Alfred Lord Milner, one of the country's most fertile imperial thinkers, a key figure in the Boer War and subsequent reconstruction of South Africa. Sensitive to political change, Milner's mission in life was to advance ways of preserving the British Empire through the principles of imperial unity and federation. In 1910, he was instrumental in inspiring a new group known as 'The Round Table', which began to publish an influential journal of the same name. Amongst its members, Leo Amery, Conservative Member of Parliament for South Birmingham from 1911 and Assistant Secretary to the War Cabinet, and Lord Robert Cecil, son of the late Conservative Prime Minister the Marquess of Salisbury and Minister of Blockade from 1916 to 1918, were to join Milner in providing crucial support for what became the Balfour Declaration, while another, Reginald Coupland, was to become a key influence on Weizmann's thinking in later years and would help to decide the future fate of Palestine.[21] In 1917, Milner's influence in the War Cabinet was at its height, with his acolytes well placed. In addition to Milner, Amery and Cecil, Weizmann was to find two other invaluable allies at the heart of the bureaucracy which was now driving the war effort. The first was a man of diverse talents and connections, the Right Honourable William Ormsby-Gore, Conservative MP for Denbigh, heir to the 3rd Baron Harlech, and husband of the daughter of the Marquess of Salisbury. More pertinently, his knowledge of the Middle East had recently been gained as an Intelligence Officer in the Arab Bureau in Cairo, and in 1917 he held the influential positions of Parliamentary Private Secretary to Milner and Assistant Secretary to the War Cabinet. Ormsby-Gore was to prove a staunch ally of Weizmann's over many years. The other was Sir Mark Sykes, also a member of the Cabinet secretariat. Sykes was a wealthy Catholic landowner, 6th Baronet and Conservative MP for Hull, who had become an expert on Turkish affairs, and a champion of its subject nationalities, the Arabs, Armenians and Jews. He was, of course, the British part of the Sykes-Picot Agreement, with which his name will always be associated, and by 1917 had a particular brief with regard to

Palestine. Weizmann was to describe him as one of Zionism's greatest finds.[22] Tragically, Sykes was to die of influenza in Paris in February 1919 when part of the British delegation to the Peace Conference, aged only 39.

Before examining the negotiations leading to the Balfour Declaration, it is as well to consider the situation which Britain and her allies found themselves in during 1917. At sea, the Battle of Jutland in 1916 had not delivered the kind of Nelsonian victory tradition demanded, while in the course of 1917 Germany's strategy of unrestricted submarine warfare threatened to choke off Britain's essential supplies. On land, the great Somme offensive launched with such high hopes in July 1916 had finally spluttered to a halt, while the French army had only held Verdun at appalling cost. The disastrous French offensive of 1917, which provoked a mutiny in their army, and the British campaign at Passchendaele were to be no more successful. The overthrow of the Tsar in March 1917, and the subsequent turn of events in Russia which resulted in the Bolshevik seizure of power in November, threatened to free veteran German and Austro-Hungarian divisions for service elsewhere. On the Italian front, October saw the Italian army almost shattered by the Austrians and Germans at Caporetto. The one positive development was the entry of the United States into the war on 6 April, but this tested the loyalty of large ethnic groups in the country, like the Irish, with their memories of the Famine and the recent Easter Rising, or the Jews, who had no reason to support a Russian alliance. In short, the British needed support from wherever it could be found. Weizmann was clear that British motives behind the Balfour Declaration combined idealism with the pressures of war, especially with regard to what was happening in the Jewish communities of Russia and the United States.[23]

In January 1917, Sykes was anxious to make contact with the leaders of British Zionism, but needed to know who they were and what they wanted. His intermediary seems to have been an anglicised Armenian, James Malcolm, who sounded out Weizmann's old adversary from the time of the Uganda controversy, Leopold Greenberg of the *Jewish Chronicle*. Somewhat surprisingly, Greenberg pointed to Weizmann and Sokolow, who had come to London the previous year and was now active in Zionist affairs. On 28 January, Malcolm introduced Weizmann and Greenberg to Sykes.[24] What Sykes wanted was a statement of the Zionist position, which is exactly what Weizmann, Sokolow and others had been working on for some time. The memorandum which he was given was called an 'Outline of Programme for the Jewish Resettlement of Palestine in Accordance with the Aspirations of the Zionist Movement'. It dealt with the future of Palestine under a Suzerain Government, which was not named but could be inferred. It called for the present and future Jewish population of Palestine to be recognised as the Jewish Nation with full civic, national and political rights. Jewish immigrants would be encouraged and helped to purchase land. The Suzerain Government was to establish a Jewish Company to foster Jewish settlement. The document also introduced a new term, coined by Sokolow, to the effect that Palestine was to be recognised as the Jewish National Home.[25] Here were the bare bones of what Weizmann was to present to the Peace Conference two years later.

Events took a decisive step forward at a meeting held on 7

> **'His Majesty's Government view with favour the establishment in Palestine of a national home for the Jewish people...'**
>
> **BALFOUR TO LORD ROTHSCHILD, 2 NOVEMBER 1917**

February 1917 at the home of Dr Moses Gaster, a long-standing English Zionist. Insisting that he was there in a private capacity, which probably fooled no one, Sykes met a group of leading Zionists, including Weizmann, Sokolow, Samuel, Lord Rothschild, James de Rothschild, Joseph Cowen, Herbert Bentwich and Harry Sacher. They were concerned to put to Sykes that what they wanted was a British protectorate which would operate under the terms of the memorandum he had received. What they did not want was for the country to be put under some form of internationalisation, which was really code for an Anglo-French condominium. Sykes assured them he was sympathetic to the idea of a Jewish Palestine and that he did not anticipate a problem with the Russians, but was wary of French intentions in the area, even though he did not consider that they had any claims in the country. The Italians would simply follow the French, he said. He was not, of course, in a position to reveal his own recent agreement with the French over the future disposition of the Turkish lands. It was agreed that Sokolow should argue the Zionist case to the French. Sykes openly put to the Zionists that they would be challenged by the growing strength of Arab nationalism, and advised that if they got Jewish support in other matters then he felt that the Arabs could be managed. This was to form an important element in Weizmann's subsequent negotiations with Feisal. From a letter to Jabotinsky sent the following day, it is clear that Weizmann was well aware of the meeting's significance, though his enthusiasm for Sykes was tempered somewhat by the feeling that the Arabs, and not the Zionists, were his priority.[26] Four days after this historic meeting, Weizmann was elected President of the English Zionist Federation, enabling him to negotiate with the government on these crucial issues from a recognised position.

From this tentative beginning, momentum then built up in the spring of 1917. What seems to have exercised the British most at this stage was the likely attitude of the French to any move over Palestine. Weizmann was warned of this by Balfour at a meeting on 22 March. It seems that Balfour took some convincing of Palestine's value to the British. His suggestion was that if they could not get an agreement with France, then the Zionists should aim for an Anglo-American condominium, an idea which did not greatly tempt Weizmann. This theme was also taken up by Lloyd George when he breakfasted with Weizmann and Scott on 3 April.[27] The real significance of these meetings was that Weizmann and Zionism were being taken seriously at the highest levels, important because large British forces were poised to advance into Palestine, but they also put into context the somewhat prolonged mission Sokolow undertook in Paris and Rome in April, May and June. It was far from a waste of time, however, since on 4 June Jules Cambon of the Foreign Ministry wrote to him expressing sympathy with his cause. This was an invaluable document to have.[28] Sokolow's lengthy absence, of course, meant that in London the spotlight fell on Weizmann.

It was at this point that Weizmann at last got wind of the Sykes-Picot Agreement through the good offices of Scott. The proposal that France should acquire part of northern Palestine, and that the rest should be internationalised ran directly counter to Zionist hopes for a British protectorate. It was clearly vital to explore this, and make it clear where the Zionists stood. Weizmann did this on 25 April at a meeting with Lord Robert Cecil, who was running the Foreign Office during Balfour's absence in the United States. There were three options for Palestine, he explained; namely, a British protectorate, an Anglo-French condominium and internationalisation. What the Jews wanted was the first of these. They trusted Britain to allow Jewish development, and grant self-government at the appropriate time. Joint rule with the French would simply lead to confusion and intrigue. Moreover, he pointed out that French colonial policy was one of assimilation to French, and Catholic, values. Internationalisation would pose a strategic threat to Egypt. Weizmann then turned to the Sykes-Picot Agreement, which he outlined with remarkable accuracy. This, he said, would combine the faults of internationalisation and a condominium, as well as partitioning Palestine. Cecil appears to have been convinced, and advised Weizmann to mobilise world Jewish opinion in support of a British protectorate.[29]

Clearly, the key to such a strategy lay with the large American Jewish community, whose leader Justice Louis D Brandeis had the ear of President Woodrow Wilson. Born in Kentucky in 1856, in 1916 Brandeis had become the first Jew to be appointed to the Supreme Court. In 1914, he had accepted the presidency of the Provisional Executive Council for General Zionist Affairs, and as such was the acknowledged leader of American Zionism. Two days before his meeting with Cecil, Weizmann had contacted Brandeis, emphasising that from the Zionist perspective it was imperative that Palestine should become a British protectorate. Amongst other things, what was concerning him were anti-annexationist views coming from the American administration. It was vital that Brandeis should meet Balfour to impress this upon him. Brandeis met Balfour on several occasions during his American visit, and the two men seem to have agreed on the need for a future British administration in Palestine.[30]

It was Brandeis in June 1917 who warned Weizmann that an American mission was coming to the Middle East, and that he should contact it. From Sykes and Ormsby-Gore he learned that this was an initiative of Henry Morgenthau, former ambassador to Constantinople, in an attempt to negotiate a separate peace with Turkey. The idea of some kind of deal which would leave the empire intact was as unwelcome to the British as it was to Weizmann, and it was Balfour who suggested that he intercept Morgenthau's party at Gibraltar and persuade him to drop the idea. In a somewhat cloak-and-dagger operation, Weizmann travelled to Gibraltar, accompanied by an armed intelligence officer, but he need not have worried, since Morgenthau soon saw the futility of the idea. In any case, the United States and Turkey were not at war. The real significance is the extent to which Weizmann was now trusted by the government, and the success of his mission certainly did his credibility no harm.[31]

While events were clearly moving Weizmann's way, his activities had rung alarm bells amongst his old adversaries in the Anglo-Jewish elite, expressed through the Conjoint Foreign Committee, which brought together the Board of Deputies of British Jews and the Anglo-Jewish Association. On 24 May 1917, they published a statement in *The Times* under the title of 'Palestine and Zionism – Views of Anglo-Jewry'. While they supported the concept of making Palestine a spiritual centre for the Jews, they were strongly opposed to Zionism's political programme, arguing that for Palestine to be regarded as a Jewish homeland would undermine what the Jews had achieved in their native countries. Their action brought to a head the latent tensions within British Jewry over the question of Zionism, with Weizmann and the Jewish peer Lord Rothschild writing letters of rebuttal to *The Times*. Weizmann's letter, which was published on 28 May, asserted in no uncertain terms that the Jews were a nationality, and added that Zionism was not seeking an exclusive position in Palestine.[32] The result of this controversy was that on 17 June the Board of Deputies voted, albeit by a narrow majority, to reject the 'Statement', and the Conjoint Foreign Committee was dissolved. This was far from the end of the campaign against a pro-Zionist policy, since a determined enemy was lying in wait in the one of the great offices of state. This was Edwin Montagu, of whose hostility to Zionism Lloyd George had warned three years before.[33]

On 13 June, Weizmann wrote to Sir Ronald Graham of the Foreign Office pressing for a British declaration of support for the Zionist position on Palestine, which he claimed, with some exaggeration, they had been negotiating for the past three years. Weizmann was at pains to point out the recent expressions of support for Zionism in influential German and Austrian newspapers.[34] By coincidence, Balfour had just received a minute recommending that the government issue an assurance of British sympathy for Zionism. He was, therefore, in a receptive mood when Weizmann, Graham and Lord Rothschild came to see him on 19 June. Balfour agreed that the time had come to issue a declaration of support, and asked them to submit a draft which he could put to the War Cabinet. He also assured them that he was opposed to an Anglo-French condominium, and that he favoured joint Anglo-American control, but felt that this would not find favour with Lloyd George or the Americans. In reporting this to his colleagues, Weizmann suggested that the draft should talk in terms of a Jewish National Home in Palestine, precisely the formula the War Cabinet ultimately agreed.[35] The drafting was done by a committee chaired by Sokolow while Weizmann was in Gibraltar.

Various versions were discussed, including one by Herbert

Sidebotham, a non-Jewish journalist on the *Manchester Guardian*, who was strongly pro-Zionist. His rather turgid version was not accepted, but is, nevertheless, well worth noting for his use of the striking phrase that the national character of the Jewish state should be as Jewish as the dominant national character of England was English. Weizmann was to utter a somewhat terser version of this when responding to a question at the Peace Conference, and its implications were to echo for years, not always to his advantage. In discussing this episode in his book *Great Britain and Palestine*, which he published in 1937, Sidebotham refrained from mentioning that he was most probably the *fons et origo* of the phrase.[36] On 18 July 1917, the agreed draft was given to Balfour by Lord Rothschild. It was admirably brief, and would have committed the British government to reconstituting Palestine as the National Home of the Jewish People, and to discussing with the Zionist Organisation how this would be done.[37] If the Zionists had reason to hope for early action, then they had not reckoned on the Byzantine ways of the British decision-making process, nor on the opposition the draft provoked.

As the Zionist draft circulated, a number of suggested amendments were put forward, the most significant being one from Milner which proposed that the declaration should commit Britain to securing a home for the Jews in Palestine.[38] The matter came before the War Cabinet on 3 September, in the absence of Lloyd George and Balfour. While Cecil and Milner and the South African General Jan Smuts were supporters of the idea, a powerful opponent had also been asked to attend. This was Edwin Montagu, Samuel's cousin, who had recently been appointed Secretary of State for India, entrusted with carrying forward the reform scheme which was to emerge under his name and that of the Viceroy, Lord

Chelmsford. Since India's wholehearted participation was vital at this stage of the war, his views mattered. Men of the Indian army formed a large part of the imperial forces in both Palestine and Mesopotamia, and it recruited heavily amongst Indian Muslims. Montagu felt passionately that the idea of a Jewish National Home undermined his status as a Jewish Englishman, and he expressed this in no uncertain terms in a memorandum which he entitled 'The Anti-Semitism of the Present Government'. The War Cabinet had before it Lord Rothschild's letter, a suggested reply by Balfour, Milner's alternative version, and Montagu's philippic against the whole idea. Montagu spoke to his memorandum, emphasising his central belief that the proposal would undermine the position of Jews everywhere. Others argued that the idea of a Jewish state in Palestine would not affect the position enjoyed by Jews in countries like Britain, but would strengthen it in countries where they did not have equal rights. Cecil argued against any postponement of the matter, pointing to the enthusiasm of the Zionist organisation, especially in the United States, and the value of having them on the Allied side. Even so, it was felt prudent to consult the other Allies, especially the Americans.[39]

With the proposed declaration seemingly hanging in the balance, Weizmann deployed all his diplomatic skills to help secure it. The first attempt to put Lord Rothschild's draft before President Woodrow Wilson through his aide Colonel Edward M House produced a rather tepid reply on 10 September, to the effect that a declaration of sympathy could be made but without any commitment. Wilson's problem was that his country was not at war with Turkey. When Weizmann learned of the tone of House's message, he immediately contacted Brandeis, emphasising the urgent need to secure Wilson's endorsement. Brandeis met House on 23 September, and the following day he telegraphed to the effect that the President was entirely sympathetic to the proposed declaration.[40]

Frustrated and somewhat perplexed by the influence Montagu was having, Weizmann was also actively lobbying on the domestic front. On 19 September, he met Balfour, who promised to use his influence with the Prime Minister, and then, a week later, he was able to snatch a few moments with Lloyd George, who issued peremptory instructions that the matter be tabled at the next Cabinet meeting.[41] With the matter now due to come back before the War Cabinet, on 3 October he and Rothschild wrote to Balfour expressing their alarm that the proposed declaration was being opposed by a prominent Jew whom they did not actually name, but who was, of course, clearly identifiable. What they sought to drive home was that the declaration had been submitted on behalf of an organisation which represented the will of a people who had the right to be regarded as a nation.[42]

The day after receiving Weizmann's letter, the War Cabinet resumed its consideration of the matter. Balfour opened the discussion by warning his colleagues that the Germans were trying to woo the Zionists. Conceding that Zionism was opposed by some wealthy British Jews, he believed it had the support of American and Russian Jews. He saw no contradiction between a national focus in Palestine and the assimilation of Jews into other countries. His justification for a declaration was that the Jews passionately wanted to regain their ancient homeland. Finally, he read the letter of support Cambon had given Sokolow, and referred to Wilson's favourable attitude, although others noted the difference in tone between the telegrams sent by House and Brandeis. Montagu responded by asserting that he was a Jewish Englishman and that the Jews were a religious community, asking how he could negotiate with the Indians if it was announced that the British government believed that his National Home was in the Turkish empire. Most native-born Jews, he claimed, were hostile to Zionism; its supporters, on the other hand, were foreign-born Jews like Weizmann, a native of Russia.

Strong opposition was also voiced by George Curzon, Earl of Kedleston, former Viceroy of India and now Leader of the House of Lords. Widely travelled in the Middle East, Curzon knew Palestine and did not think much of its potential as a future home for the Jews. More importantly, he asked how it was proposed to get rid of what he called the country's Muslim majority. The government should have nothing to do with the proposed declaration, he concluded. Knowing where the arguments were likely to go, Milner tried to square the circle in advance of the meeting. Just before the start of the War Cabinet, he asked Amery to draft a formula which might satisfy both the Jewish and pro-Arab critics. Amery's hastily-composed text added to Milner's earlier draft that nothing should be done to prejudice the rights of the existing non-Jewish population of Palestine or those enjoyed by Jews in other countries. It was agreed to put this to Wilson as well as to the Zionists and their opponents.[43]

Faced with this fresh delay, Weizmann once again moved to secure the backing he needed. On 9 October, he cabled Brandeis with the new version of the proposed declaration, stressing the need to secure Wilson's endorsement as well as that of the American Zionists.[44] In fact, House had already received it from Balfour, and the American embassy in London had also sent it direct to Wilson. On 16 October, House informed the British of Wilson's approval, with the proviso that it not be made public and on the following day Brandeis was able to confirm this to Weizmann. The American Zionists made two suggested amendments to the proposed text, both of which found their way into the final version.[45] Meanwhile, Weizmann was also mobilising Zionist opinion at home, with some 300 synagogues and societies registering their support for a declaration.[46]

When the War Cabinet met for what proved to be its final discussion of the topic on 31 October, Balfour met his critics head-on. He emphasised the propaganda they could conduct in Russia and the United States, since the majority of Jews in these countries were behind Zionism. Once again, he was dismissive of the assimilationist fear of double allegiance. Montagu was not there to counter this, since he had left for India. As to Curzon's point about the unsuitability of Palestine, he claimed that if the country were properly developed it could sustain a much larger population, an argument which Weizmann was to use in the years to come. As to what was meant by the term 'National Home', his argument was interesting, since he said it did not necessarily mean the early establishment of a Jewish state, but would be some kind of British, American or other protectorate which could become a focus of Jewish national life. Curzon, the only one who had actually seen the country at first hand, remained pessimistic, but was grudgingly prepared to acknowledge the political value of what was being proposed. The way was now open for the Cabinet to authorise the Declaration, which was issued in a letter from Balfour to Lord Rothschild on 2 November:

'His Majesty's Government view with favour the establishment in Palestine of a national home for the Jewish people, and will use its best endeavours to facilitate the achievement of this object, it being clearly understood that nothing shall be done which may prejudice the civil and religious rights of existing non-Jewish communities in Palestine, or the rights and political status enjoyed by Jews in any other country'.[47]

Weizmann later recalled that at the conclusion of the Cabinet meeting, Sykes brought the Declaration out to him with the exclamation that it was a boy. If it was not quite all that Weizmann had hoped for, its birth was more down to him than anyone else, and he knew that history was in the making, referring to it in a letter to Rothschild as the Magna Carta of the Jews.[48] That evening, his wife later recorded, the Weizmanns and some friends formed a circle at his home and danced a Hassidic dance in celebration. A month later, there was a large demonstration in London of Jewish gratitude for the Declaration, which was addressed by Cecil, Samuel, Sykes and Ormsby-Gore, as well as Weizmann. If the British government had hoped to influence the course of events in Russia, the Declaration might have succeeded, since Russian Jews were, indeed, stirred by it, but by then the second revolution had robbed it of any real potential.[49] The Declaration was followed, on 1 February 1918, by a letter from Stephen Pichon of the Foreign Ministry to Sokolow, assuring him that the French were in agreement with the British over what he rather tepidly termed a 'Jewish establishment' in Palestine, a phrase which allowed later interpretation.[50]

Balfour and Weizmann in Jerusalem in April 1925.

II

The Paris Peace Conference

4

The Paris Peace Conference

Weizmann could have been forgiven for feeling euphoric about the way events had turned out, especially since the Balfour Declaration was followed by General Allenby's victorious entry into Jerusalem on 11 December 1917, but 1918 was to expose something of the reality of what the creation of the National Home would entail. For much of the year he was in Palestine as Chairman of a Zionist Commission, which the British government suggested in December 1917. Its purpose was to establish a link between the Jews and the British military authorities, but it was also to co-ordinate relief for the Jewish population, help with the rebuilding of Jewish institutions, much needed as a result of the war, and to make political connections with the Arabs. Its terms of reference were later expanded to include Weizmann's favourite project of a Jewish university. Although it was intended that the Commission's membership should include Jews from the principal Allied countries, the situation in Russia precluded this, and the Americans declined to take part since they were not at war with Turkey. The Italian member was Angelo Levi-Bianchini, a naval officer, and the French appointed the distinguished scholar Sylvain Levi, Professor of Sanskrit at the elite College de France, who, however, was not a Zionist. Weizmann's other colleagues were Joseph Cowen, Dr David Eder and Leon Simon, while his old friend Ormsby-Gore acted as his liaison officer.[1]

Weizmann left for the Middle East in early March, having first been received in audience by King George V. Given wartime conditions, it was a far from easy journey, and it was the end of the month before he arrived in Cairo *en route* to Palestine. His first contact with the High Commissioner in Egypt, Sir Reginald Wingate, and his Chief Political Officer Brigadier-General Gilbert Clayton, seemed positive enough, though the question of Arab attitudes to possible Zionist intentions was raised.[2] Weizmann finally arrived at Tel Aviv on 4 April, and was immediately welcomed by Allenby at his nearby headquarters. While Allenby impressed him, Weizmann quickly concluded that the military authorities had no real grasp of the Balfour Declaration, and that they were very conscious of the position of the Arabs.[3] With his army planning its next advance, it was obvious that Allenby would not want a restive Palestine at his back, and Weizmann was alive to that. Disquieting signs were there, as he soon found out. On 11 April, the Military Governor of Jerusalem, Colonel Ronald Storrs, attended a function in the city at which speakers asserted Palestine's Arab identity. Storrs later recalled the Arab reactions to the Balfour Declaration, which were that they had been relegated to the position of 'non-Jewish communities', and that there had been no reference to their political rights.[4]

On 18 April, Weizmann wrote home, giving Vera his thoughts on what he had seen. Jerusalem had impressed him no better than it had on first acquaintance. Once again, he lamented its lack of Jewish institutions and the nature of its Jewish inhabitants. The Jewish colonies elsewhere, on the other hand, excited his keen admiration, despite the effects of over three years of war. What was obviously giving him real cause for concern was the partiality of the British military for the Arabs. He confided in Brandeis that the Arabs believed it was the British government's intention to set up a Jewish government and expel them, and that, as a result, they were highly suspicious of the Commission.[5] With the issue of Arab attitudes now uppermost in his mind, Weizmann responded positively to a suggestion from Clayton that he should meet Feisal, Britain's principal Arab ally.

The journey to the camp of Feisal's Arab army was something of an adventure, in the course of which Ormsby-Gore came down with dysentery. Weizmann was able to approach close to the Turkish lines, watch Feisal's army at work, and witness T E Lawrence's preparations for his raids on the Hejaz railway. The meeting with Feisal went well. Weizmann explained the nature of the Zionist Commission, said that they wished to allay the fears of the Arabs, and hoped for Feisal's support. Feisal's answers seemed to indicate that he looked favourably on what he had heard, and Weizmann made his way back to Palestine convinced that he had enlisted the sympathy of the real leader of Arab nationalism. He wrote to Vera that Feisal held no high opinion of the Arabs of Palestine.[6] There is no doubt that Weizmann came away from this meeting with the belief that here, at last, was the Arab leader with whom he could work. Subsequent events were to prove him both right and wrong. The fact that he had engaged so positively with Feisal led to the conclusion of the Feisal-Weizmann Agreement of January 1919, which strengthened his hand at the Peace Conference. But events were to show that the leadership of the Arab national movement, and particularly of the Palestinian Arabs, did not lie with Feisal, and that Weizmann was building too many hopes on their relationship. In a letter to Balfour on 17 July, he enthusiastically set out the prospects should Feisal enter Damascus, dismissing the Arabs of Palestine as of merely local significance.[7] Before leaving Palestine, Weizmann was to see the realisation of a project which he had embraced and encouraged for many years. On 24 July, in a ceremony attended by Allenby, Weizmann spoke at the laying of the foundation-stone of the future Hebrew University on Mount Scopus.[8]

His return from Palestine in October allowed Weizmann no respite, rather the contrary since the war was clearly entering its final phase at bewildering speed, especially in the Middle East where Allenby's forces had conquered all of Syria and Palestine by the end of the month. With the future of Palestine now likely to be at Britain's disposal, he formed a small group chaired by Herbert Samuel, consisting of Sir Alfred Mond, Sokolow and himself, charged with producing a scheme whereby the Jewish position in the country could go forward under British trusteeship. Ormsby-Gore was also associated with its work.[9] Weizmann also embarked upon a flurry of meetings with leading politicians, including Balfour, Cecil, Sykes, Ormsby-Gore, Samuel, Lord Reading, Lord Bryce and General Smuts, as well as key figures in British intelligence, and T E Lawrence and Commander David Hogarth, former head of the Arab Bureau. The focus of his discussions with Cecil, Lawrence and Hogarth seems to have been the need to maintain close relations with Feisal, which clearly needed a sensitive touch. The level of access he enjoyed at this pivotal time was, once again, of incalculable value to the Zionist movement.[10]

Also anxious to keep his American colleagues in close step with what he was doing, Weizmann explained the position at some length to Brandeis on 29 October 1918. What clearly concerned him was that in view of the rapid turn of events in the war, Zionism was hardly a priority for the Allied leaders. Even so, the situation in the Middle East had its own momentum. In the course of October, Feisal had set up his government in Damascus, which Weizmann naturally viewed as a positive development, explaining to Brandeis how the Hashemite leader had been prepared to acknowledge Palestine as a Jewish sphere of influence in return for technical and economic assistance to the Arab states. What he portrayed as a division of the Middle East between the Hashemites and the Zionists, he feared was being undermined by the details, which were now emerging, of the Sykes-Picot Agreement, resented as it was by the Arabs. But he was also concerned by reports of growing Arab hostility to the Jews in Palestine, and by the extent of pogroms in the disintegrating empires of Central and Eastern Europe. In a letter to his friend David Eder in Tel Aviv, he confided his fear that if they did not secure Palestine these communities might be exterminated.[11] His concern that the American Zionists should put their full weight behind any representation to a peace conference was repeated in a message to Brandeis sent on Armistice Day. On that historic day he had lunch with Lloyd George, arranged, it seems, by his old friend C P Scott.[12]

Meanwhile, what was of the essence was an agreed statement of what the Zionists wanted to come out of any peace conference, and given the disparate nature of the movement, stretched as it was across several jurisdictions, this was not as straightforward as it might have seemed. In the circumstances, it was vital to put down a marker about what the Zionists felt should happen during this crucial interim period. After meetings with Balfour and Cecil, on 1 November 1918 Weizmann submitted to the latter a 10-point document setting this out. Acknowledging that control would be in the hands of the British, the document requested that the work of the Zionist Commission be allowed to continue and that it be made the advisory body to the military administration on matters relating to the Jewish inhabitants. In addition, the military was to assist the Commission in organising the Jewish population and encouraging Jewish participation in administration. In a matter close to Weizmann's heart, the commission was to be permitted to carry out preparatory work for the Hebrew University on Mount Scopus. Crucially, a land commission was to be created, including Zionist Commission members, with a view to reviewing land tenure and ownership, including an examination of land registers and a possible modification of existing land law.[13]

Significant as this statement was, it could be nothing more than a holding document until Samuel's committee had completed its work on a definitive statement of Zionist aims which would be placed in the hands of the Peace Conference. A draft was ready by the end of November, and Weizmann, understandably anxious to sound out British reactions to what they would be proposing, sent copies to General Clayton in Palestine and, crucially, to Balfour. At a meeting with Balfour on 4 December, Weizmann proposed that the Peace Conference should declare Palestine to be a Jewish country under a trustee. He then revealed that they would be asking for Britain to be that trustee, and confirmed that they would want to see a Jewish population of some four to five million being built up over the next 25 years. The interview was positive, with Balfour indicating his broad agreement with what was going to be proposed, and assuring Weizmann that it did not deviate from his November 1917 Declaration.[14]

However reassuring this might be, Weizmann still needed to secure other flanks, not least with Feisal who was also expected to press his claims before the Peace Conference. The two leaders met in London on 11 December 1918, with Lawrence acting as interpreter. Feisal began by denouncing the Sykes-Picot Agreement, a sentiment in which Weizmann concurred. He then asked for an outline of the Zionist programme. Weizmann's reply was remarkably candid, saying that they expected the Conference and Feisal to acknowledge the rights of the Jews to Palestine. They would request that the country be put under British trusteeship, with a government in which the Jews would share. He also confirmed that they would request a reform of the land laws in order to permit the colonisation of four to five million Jews, while safeguarding the rights of the Arab peasantry, and reassured Feisal that there was no intention to interfere with the Muslim Holy Places. For his part, Feisal responded that he would seek to reassure the Peace Conference that the Zionist and Arab movements were in harmony, and that he would support the Jewish position.[15] The essence of this conversation was embodied in a document drawn up between the two leaders and signed on 3 January 1919. In what was to become known as the Feisal-Weizmann Agreement, the two agreed to promote the close co-operation of the Arab State and Palestine, the boundaries of which would be defined after the Peace Conference. The constitution and administration of Palestine would allow for the implementation of the Balfour Declaration. Large-scale Jewish immigration into Palestine was to be encouraged, while the rights of the Arab farmers would be protected. Provision was to be made for the free exercise of religion, and the Muslim Holy Places were to be under Muslim control. A commission of experts sent to Palestine by the Zionist Organisation was also to report on how the Arab State might be developed. Finally, the parties pledged to work together on all these matters before the Peace Conference. Feisal did, however, enter an important caveat, of which there are two rather different versions. In the rather opaque translation made by T E Lawrence, Feisal recorded that if changes were made to the establishment of the Arabs then he could not be answerable for any failure to carry out the agreement. In the version published in 1938 by the Palestinian historian George Antonius, Feisal was more specific, making the agreement absolutely dependent upon the implementation of Arab independence. In fact, the meaning is clear enough, and the subsequent collapse of Feisal's hopes in Syria rendered the agreement meaningless; but it is interesting that Feisal made it, just the same.[16]

In anticipation of the forthcoming Peace Conference, Weizmann went to Paris at the beginning of January 1919 as part of the Zionist Mission which had been invited to present the movement's case, staying at the Hotel Plaza on the avenue Montaigne.[17] An early sign that things might go his way came at a meeting with Colonel House. Weizmann left with the clear impression that the Americans were sympathetic to the Zionist position, not least since House assured him that he had recently been briefed on the issues by Balfour. In a letter to his wife, he confided in her that the Americans favoured a Jewish Palestine under British auspices, the essence of the position he was preparing to put to the conference. House also promised to arrange a meeting with President Wilson, which took place on 14 January. The fact that Weizmann had that level of access was in itself significant, and must have done his credibility no harm in his uneasy relations with the American Zionists.[18] His chief concern was ensuring that the statement of policy which was to be presented to the Conference was as realistic as possible, especially given the rather different perspectives of the various Zionist groups and his contacts in British government circles. Reconciling these views was by no means straightforward, as it turned out.

For some time Weizmann had been uneasy about the attitude of the British military administration in Palestine, which he felt was too inclined to take the Arab side. It was, therefore, important to seek the views of General Sir Arthur Money, Chief Administrator in Palestine, who was then in London. Money's reaction was that the Arabs would react against the proposals in the draft document, not least where they would affect the land. In reply, Weizmann argued that unless the Jews secured a home they would be faced with a catastrophe. He also asserted the historic right of the Jews to Palestine, which, he said, was not invalidated by the fact that their expulsion had happened 2,000 years before. On the land question, he claimed that what they wanted was to break up the large estates in favour of small farmers, by implication Jewish, though this was not stated.[19] But by 3 February 1919, the final text of this key document had been agreed. Much would turn on it, and its content was to underpin, in no small measure, the nature of the subsequent British Mandate for Palestine.

The 'Statement of the Zionist Organisation regarding Palestine' was signed by Lord Rothschild, by Weizmann and Sokolow on behalf of the Zionist Organisation and of the Jewish population of Palestine, by Israel Rosoff for the Russian Zionist Organisation, and by Julian Mack, Stephen Wise, Harry Friedenwald, Jacob de Haas, Mary Fels, Louis

Robison and Bernard Flexner for the Zionist Organisation of America. There was a noticeable absence of any French Jewish signatory. In its preamble the document asked that the Conference recognise the Jews' historic title to Palestine and their right to have their National Home there. The newly-formed League of Nations was to have sovereignty over Palestine, governed by Great Britain as its Mandatory.

The choice of Britain rested on what the document claimed was the special relationship it had with Zionism, as evidenced by the El Arish Offer, the Uganda Offer and the Balfour Declaration. Moreover, the Jews liked the way in which Britain had approached colonial government. The British were to create the necessary conditions for the creation of the National Home, but, in an interesting move beyond the terms of the Balfour Declaration, the document also looked forward to the eventual creation of an autonomous Commonwealth. In order to do that, Britain was to promote Jewish immigration and settlement while safeguarding the rights of the non-Jewish population, work together with a Jewish council, and give that council priority where public works and natural resources were concerned. On the critical question of land, the Mandatory was to appoint a commission, with Jewish representation, which would have the power of compulsory purchase, as well as making available state land and what it described as inadequately cultivated land, though the position of the existing population was to be protected. There was to be no discrimination on racial or religious grounds. The boundary of Palestine was to lie east of the river Jordan close to the line of the Hejaz railway, and include the river headwaters on Mount Hermon in the north.

The document was at pains to justify the nature of the Jews' claims to Palestine, notably that it was their historic home from which they had been violently expelled, but to which they had always hoped to return. In addition, Palestine would provide a refuge for Jews living under harsh conditions in Eastern Europe, even though it was conceded that the country was unable to take in more than a minority of them. Finally, the document pointed to what it claimed was the desolate condition of the land, which could only be developed through Jewish enterprise, as evidenced by the success of the existing settlements. These Jewish claims to Palestine had been recognised in the Balfour Declaration, and then supported by the French, Italian, American, Japanese, Greek, Serbian, Chinese and Siamese governments.[20]

The Conference had opened in Paris on 18 January 1919 under the presidency of the veteran French Prime Minister, Georges Clemenceau. While a wide variety of countries was present in Paris, the Supreme Council, consisting of the leaders of the United Kingdom, France, the United States, Italy and Japan, represented the principal victors. Although Palestine was far from the top of their agenda, it was to the advantage of Weizmann and the Zionists that the British Empire's representatives on the Council were Lloyd George and Balfour. The Conference's dominant personalities were Clemenceau, Lloyd George and Wilson.

The Zionist delegation was scheduled to present its case before the Supreme Council on 28 February 1919, but on the 26th Weizmann and Sokolow were informed that their meeting was being brought forward to the next day. The practical effect of this was that Jacob de Haas, who was to represent the American Zionists but who was still in London, was unable arrive in time. Much worse from Weizmann's perspective was the unwelcome news that the French Foreign Ministry was inviting two representatives of the French Jewish community. The first of these, André Spire, was a distinguished civil servant of noted Zionist sympathies. But his colleague, Sylvain Levi was much more problematic. Not only did Levi come from a strongly assimilationist background hostile to Zionism, but he and Weizmann had crossed swords the previous year on the Zionist Commission. Members of the British and American delegations professed ignorance over Levi's invitation, but an attempt by Weizmann to lobby against him was unsuccessful. According to Weizmann's account, however, Levi was annoyed at not being trusted, and promised to say nothing against Zionism.[21]

The Zionist Mission which presented itself before the Supreme Council in the Quai d'Orsay on the afternoon of 27 February 1919 consisted of Weizmann, Sokolow, Ussishkin, Spire and Levi. Present to hear them were the Foreign Ministers Stephen Pichon of France, Baron Sonnino of Italy and Baron Makino of Japan, as well as the American Secretary of State Robert Lansing. The British Empire was represented by Balfour and Milner, who, of course, had the arguments at their fingertips, while Ormsby-Gore was also present for this particular session. The Zionists could be assured of a sympathetic hearing and reception from the British members, while Pichon, too, was familiar with the issue, having signed the French government's declaration of 14 February 1918, and personally assured Sokolow of its support for the British government's position. In his autobiography, Weizmann recollected that Clemenceau had been present for the early part of the hearing, and it seems that he did stay for a short time.[22]

The Zionist case was opened, with his customary gravitas, by Sokolow, who requested that he submit to the Council the 'Statement of the Zionist Organisation regarding Palestine', adding that the delegation had come to assert the historic rights of the Jews to Palestine where they had created their civilisation prior to the Dispersion. Conceding the comfortable position of the Jewish communities of France, Britain, Italy and the United States, a key point in view of the nature of his audience, he nevertheless argued that they represented only a minority of a much greater world Jewish population whose needs could only be met through the establishment of a home. Sokolow then rehearsed the principal recommendations of the 'Statement' he had distributed; namely, that the Jews' historic title to Palestine be recognised together with the right to have a National Home there; that the League of Nations be granted sovereignty over Palestine with Britain as the Mandatory power; and that Palestine be governed in such a way as to secure the Jewish National Home with the possibility of this leading to an autonomous commonwealth which would have due regard to the rights of the country's non-Jewish population and the status of the Jews in other countries. Weizmann's recollection was that his colleague had made a real impression on his listeners.[23]

It was now Weizmann's turn. While he was experienced in dealing with senior British politicians and public servants, this was his debut before such an international gathering, and his main concern was to convince them of the practicalities of the Zionist endeavour. He brought with him his recent experience as president of the 1918 Zionist Commission in Palestine. Beginning by highlighting the pre-war sufferings of the six to seven million Russian Jews, he argued that these had continued under the new regime. This would result in an increase in Jewish emigration, but he predicted that the capacity of Western Europe and the United States to absorb immigrants would bring them under increasing scrutiny; in view of what was to happen to American immigration legislation in the early 1920s, which introduced strict ethnic quotas, he was accurate enough. He then turned to the crucial question of Palestine. Acknowledging that there were between 600,000 and 700,000 existing inhabitants, he argued that this represented a population density of 10 to 15 per square kilometre, which he compared with 160 per square kilometre in Lebanon. As a result, he argued that some four to five million could be settled without detriment to the rights of the existing population. Such was the essence of his case. In order to promote this settlement, the proposed Mandatory Power would promote Jewish immigration and settlement, while safeguarding the rights of the existing population; work to develop the National Home in co-operation with a council representing the Jews of Palestine and elsewhere; and give that council priority in the development of Palestine's natural resources. Weizmann concluded by referring to the one million Jews who, he claimed, were waiting to come to Palestine, emphasising that the support of the Great Powers would be needed for this to be done.[24]

Ussishkin, who spoke as President of the South Russian Jewish National Assembly representing some three million Jews, was brief, and contented himself with supporting what Sokolow and Weizmann had said. He was followed by Spire, who, while saying that he spoke on behalf of the French Zionists, conceded that they were a minority of French Jews. So far, all four had been remarkably succinct. Not so Levi, who addressed the Council for some 20 minutes, managing to undermine much of what the others had said. From the start he made it clear that he was not a Zionist, and that while a Jew by origin he was French. Even so, the first part of what he had to say did not seem greatly at odds with what had gone before. He, too, stressed the suffering of the Jews of Central and Eastern Europe, insisting that they dreamt of Palestine as the one place where their sense of nationality could be developed. He then proceeded to demonstrate that the Zionist movement had already created a foundation for further development through the fostering of the Jewish settlements which Rothschild had encouraged, as well as the opening of schools. Zionism's task, he argued, was to direct Jewish migration from Eastern Europe to Palestine.

At that point the tone of his submission changed abruptly. He said that he would now address the practical difficulties with the frankness of an historian. In the first place he pointed to the size of Palestine compared with the millions of Eastern European Jews who might go there. The country's present population was 600,000 to 700,000 Arabs, and he did not feel that an equal number of Jews could be accommodated at the standard of living they had experienced in Europe. He then turned to the nature of the prospective Jewish settlement, drawn as it would be from countries where they had been persecuted. They would, he warned, bring dangerous passions to Palestine, which, in a curious turn of phrase, he said would become a concentration camp for Jews. A further problem would be the merging of Jews from such a diverse group of countries into a single nationality, something with which the Peace Conference would be familiar. The Zionist solution to this dilemma was to be the formation of an International Jewish Council with responsibilities for Palestine, but as a Frenchman of Jewish origin he feared the dual citizenship which this might imply. Turning to the principles of the French Revolution, he then argued that as the Jews had campaigned for equal rights in the countries they inhabited, it would be shocking if they claimed an exceptional position in Palestine. The most he would concede, it appeared, was the creation of a Jewish committee to organise immigration and look after economic and social affairs in Palestine but with no political function. Notwithstanding the fact that his lengthy discourse had gone far to undo much of what had gone before, he ended by reminding the council of the Jews' contribution to civilisation and the further contributions they might make by the shores of the Mediterranean.[25]

There is no doubt that the nature of Levi's submission threw the rest of the delegation into confusion, but after a hasty consultation they decided against entering into a public debate with him before the Council.[26] They were rescued from their dilemma by Lansing who asked Weizmann whether the term 'Jewish National Home' meant an autonomous Jewish government. He replied that they did not want the latter but rather an administration, which, under a Mandatory, would be able to build up Jewish institutions. Over time, a sense of nationality would grow so that, in his striking phrase, Palestine would become as Jewish as America was American or England was English.

Made impromptu in reply to Lansing's question, this concept was to enter the political lexicon over the next few years, not always to Weizmann's advantage. Weizmann then seized the opportunity to refute Levi. Since the International Jewish Council would have no political function, the matter of dual allegiance to which the Frenchman had alluded would not arise. Conceding Levi's point that Palestine as it then existed could not absorb large numbers, he made the obvious riposte that it was their purpose to transform the country in the manner of California or the French colony of Tunisia. In the latter, he instanced that there were eight million olive trees compared with 45,000 in 1882.

> 'Thus it would build up gradually a nationality, and so make Palestine as Jewish as America is American, or England English.'
>
> **CHAIM WEIZMANN, 27 FEBRUARY 1919**

To achieve this kind of change would be difficult, he admitted, but not as bad as the problems of the Jews of Eastern Europe. Finally, in a clear stroke against the assimilationist position Levi had represented so vigorously, he claimed that he spoke for 96 per cent of the Jews of the world.[27] The delegation then left. Balfour's secretary came out to pass on his congratulations. Weizmann pointedly refused Levi's proffered hand, and accused him of betrayal. The two men never spoke again.[28] An exultant Weizmann confided in his wife that it had been the most triumphant moment of his life.[29]

The day after his appearance before the Council, Weizmann sought to reinforce his message in an interview with the British journalist Walter Duranty, which appeared in the *New York Times* on 3 March. He repeated what he had said about the Jews' right to reconstitute their National Home in Palestine under British trusteeship, but he also used the interview to refine his reply to Lansing with regard to the future shape of a Jewish polity in the country. There would not, he emphasised, be the immediate creation of a Jewish state or commonwealth; rather, he conceded that for some time to come the Jews would be a minority in Palestine and that they would not be imposing their will on the majority.[30] Generally, reactions to what had happened were positive. The French press was overwhelmingly supportive, and André Tardieu issued a statement to the effect that France would not oppose a British trusteeship for Palestine nor a Jewish state, a term which the Zionist delegation had not used. A meeting with Lansing on 29 February clearly went well. The only immediately discordant note came in a newspaper interview with Feisal, which Weizmann and his colleagues sought to counter. The result was a letter sent by Feisal on 3 March 1919 to the American Zionist Felix Frankfurter. He recalled his earlier contacts with Weizmann, assuring Frankfurter of his deepest sympathy with Zionism, whose proposals he described as modest. He did allude to difficulties which were arising in Palestine, but dismissed these as matters of detail rather than of principle. The Jews would be welcome, he claimed.[31] Two days later, Weizmann gave a very full account of his meeting with the Peace Conference to the International Zionist Conference in London. His speech included his spat with Levi and his response to Lansing's intervention to the effect that Palestine would become as Jewish as England was English. He also read verbatim Feisal's letter to Frankfurter. Overall, his speech was one of reassurance, even euphoric in tone, and he concluded by declaring that in principle the Jewish National Home was a *fait accompli*.[32]

Notwithstanding the tone of Feisal's assurances to Frankfurter, there were distinct signs that the Arabs of Palestine were becoming increasingly uneasy about Zionist intentions. At a meeting on 1 April and in a subsequent letter, Balfour seemingly warned Weizmann that the activities of the Zionists in Palestine were creating tensions with the Arab population. In reply, Weizmann conceded both that he was worried by what was happening, which he believed was being directed from Damascus, and by what some Zionists had been saying about the nature of the National Home. He tried to reassure Balfour that the movement was committed to the terms of the 1917 Declaration, which promised to safeguard the rights of the non-Jewish population, and of Feisal's continuing support. He argued that the unrest in the country would continue until the mandate was decided. But he was also worried by the attitude of the British military administrators in Palestine, who, he implied, did not share the pro-Zionist sympathies of Balfour and Allenby, and asked that new men be put in place.[33] That British concerns over the situation in Palestine were not confined to Balfour was confirmed on 12 April at meetings with Lloyd George and with Sir Eric Drummond. The Prime Minister's suggestion was that Weizmann should go to Palestine. In the discussion with Drummond, Weizmann asserted that Palestine was a Jewish rather than an Arab country, and must have been reassured when told that Balfour shared this view, but he was warned that they had to be careful.[34]

In the weeks and months that followed, the affairs of Palestine inevitably receded, since the terms of the German settlement were uppermost in the minds of the Allied leaders. It was inevitably a frustrating time for Weizmann, since it was still uncertain whether a Mandate for Palestine would be awarded to Britain, or, indeed, if it would accept it. French ambitions in the region were still active, and Feisal was apparently working hard to consolidate his position in Damascus, where he returned in April. Events on the ground had their own momentum, far removed from the rarefied atmosphere of Paris. It was soon clear that cracks were appearing in Feisal's apparent *entente* with Weizmann. On 16 May, Lieutenant-Colonel Cornwallis, Deputy Chief Political Officer at Damascus, reported that Feisal was beginning to realise that the question of relations between the Palestinians and the Zionists was not as simple as he had thought. Cornwallis also forwarded a translation of Feisal's speech to Syrian notables in Damascus on 9 May in which he rallied support for Arab independence, expressions of solidarity coming from, amongst others, a delegate from Palestine.[35] Weizmann's suspicions about the sympathies of the British military in Palestine were far from groundless. On 5 May, General Gilbert Clayton, Chief Political Officer on Allenby's staff, forwarded a report by General Arthur Money, Chief Administrator in Palestine, in which he stressed the degree of opposition to the Zionist programme which had been presented to the Peace Conference, concluding that as a result the population would prefer an American or French Mandate to that of Britain. Endorsing Money's appreciation, Clayton added that 'fear and distrust of Zionist aims grows daily and no amount of persuasion or propaganda will dispel it'. On seeing this, Balfour suggested to Curzon that Samuel be consulted on how the hostility to Zionism could be allayed by the administration.[36]

> 'Fear and distrust of Zionist aims grows daily and no amount of persuasion or propaganda will dispel it.'
>
> GENERAL GILBERT CLAYTON, 5 MAY 1919

Where this new-found activism was coming from was explained in a report entitled 'The Arab Movement and

Zionism', which was compiled by Major J N Camp, Assistant Political Officer in Jerusalem, on 12 August and forwarded to Curzon. Camp listed six Arab societies in Palestine, some of whose members he dismissed as 'ruffians and cut-throats', but others he knew were men of substance. With hindsight, what he had to say about *El Nadi el Arabi* (The Arab Club), which he identified as being dominated by the Husayni family, and strongly opposed to Zionism is particularly interesting. Haj Amin al-Husayni, who was soon to come into prominence, was identified as among the leaders, though not, in Camp's view as violent as some others. His overall conclusion was that 'practically all Moslems and Christians of any importance in Palestine are anti-Zionists, and bitterly so', and that 'Dr. Weizmann's agreement with Emir Feisal is not worth the paper it is written on or the energy wasted in the conversation to make it'. So far his analysis might be held to sustain Weizmann's growing suspicion that the British military in Palestine was pro-Arab, but Camp's conclusions were rather more nuanced than that. He recommended that trouble might be averted by peaceful Jewish penetration, 'without the blaring of trumpets and without any special privileges such as Dr. Weizmann and other official Zionists desire'. Britain could adopt a Mandate for Palestine,

Haj Amin al-Husayni (1895–1974) was a member of one of Jerusalem's most prominent families. A former Ottoman officer, he joined the Arab Revolt in the First World War, and came into political prominence in 1920 with the Nabi Musa protests in Jerusalem, for which he was sentenced to 10 years *in absentia*. The following year, Sir Herbert Samuel pardoned him, appointing him Mufti of Jerusalem. In 1936, he became head of the Arab Higher Committee at the time of the uprising against the Mandate, and went into exile. In 1941, he met both Mussolini and Hitler, and later helped recruit Balkan Muslims into the Waffen SS, acts which did little to help the Palestinian case after 1945. Dedicated to the Palestinian cause, he died in Beirut in 1974.

but not a Zionist Palestine. Immigrants could come in on a yearly basis as long as the land could sustain them, a policy Britain was to adopt before too long. If this occurred, the Arabs could not object if the Jews gained supremacy in 20 or 30 years, he felt.[37]

This increasingly bleak analysis of the prospects for Zionism was to be reinforced from an unexpected quarter, the conclusions of the American King-Crane Commission. This mission had its origins in a discussion of the Supreme Council of the Peace Conference on 20 March when Wilson suggested sending an Inter-Allied Commission to the country. After initially signalling their acceptance, Lloyd George and Clemenceau backed away from the idea, but the Americans went ahead without them at the end of May. The two commissioners were Dr Henry C King, President of Oberlin College in Ohio, and Charles R Crane, a Chicago manufacturer, Wilson apparently believing that that lack of knowledge of the country would be of advantage to them. Their report, submitted on 28 August, recommended a united Syria and Palestine under Feisal, with the Mandate taken up by the United States, or, failing that, Great Britain. Since it was quickly pigeonholed, it might have merited a brief footnote, if that, but for what it revealed about the political temper of Palestine. Comparing the Balfour Declaration with what they had heard from the Zionist Commission in Palestine, the two commissioners reported that a National Home was not the same as a Jewish State, nor could the latter be brought about except by trespassing on the rights of the existing non-Jewish communities. The Zionist representatives, they said, were looking forward to the dispossession of the non-Jewish inhabitants through purchase. Referring to Wilson's speech of 4 July 1918, in which he had emphasised the need for the acceptance of any settlement by the people concerned, they reported that nine-tenths of the population were opposed to Zionism. British officers they had consulted had said that the Zionist programme could only be carried out by force of arms. They also dismissed the Zionist claim to Palestine on the grounds that the Jews had lived there two thousand years before. While it has been suggested that the two men were the victims of propaganda, their report broadly confirms what was being heard from other sources.[38]

While such investigations were on-going, the task before Weizmann and his colleagues was clearly to ensure that the British moved swiftly to confirm their commitment to a Palestinian Mandate and implementation of the Balfour Declaration. On 31 May, Curzon followed Balfour's advice and communicated to Samuel the gist of Clayton's pessimistic analysis of the situation in the country, and asked him how he thought the administration in Palestine could counter the opposition to Zionism. Samuel, Weizmann and Sokolow conferred, and on 6 June Weizmann submitted their reply in Samuel's name. It accused the administration in Palestine of not conducting its policies in accordance with the Balfour Declaration, and that, as a result, the Arabs had been encouraged in the belief that they could force the British to abandon it through agitation. The answer, it was argued, was to convince them that the matter was 'a *chose jugee* and that continued agitation could only be to the detriment of the country and would certainly be without result'. Hence, the government should send definite instructions to the local administration that Britain would accept the Mandate for Palestine and that its terms would include the substance of the Balfour Declaration.[39]

Balfour seemed to have taken the point that something

now needed to be done, especially since the Conference was winding down, and that Wilson and Lloyd George would be leaving Paris shortly. On 26 June, two days before the signing of the Treaty, Balfour addressed a memorandum to the Prime Minister, outlining his views on the shape of a Turkish settlement. This document stated that all the Arab territories should be separated from the empire and put under Mandatories. France should get the Mandate for Syria, Britain that for Mesopotamia, and Palestine should be awarded either to the United States or Britain. Curzon endorsed this, with the proviso that he did not think Congress would permit any American Mandates.[40] With his business before the Conference concluded, Weizmann had left for London. There he kept up the pressure on Whitehall, meeting Graham at the Foreign Office on 2 July. Denouncing the current administration in Palestine in no uncertain terms for its pro-Arab bias, he accused Allenby of taking no interest in the country and Clayton of being weak, while particularly castigating Ronald Storrs, the Governor of Jerusalem. In his minute on Graham's report, Curzon sourly observed that the Zionists were reaping the harvest they had sowed.[41] Weizmann was also conferring with Cecil with a view to pushing ahead with the Mandate. On 24 July, a somewhat mystified Philip Noel Baker, Secretary to the Commission on Mandates, wrote to the Foreign Office that Cecil and Weizmann had agreed that a draft Mandate should be drawn up and published. Balfour was non-committal, minuting that any draft Mandate should be referred to him.[42] Even so, Weizmann's campaign seems to have succeeded, since on 4 August Curzon telegraphed Colonel John French, acting Chief Political Officer, instructions for the guidance of the administration: 'His Majesty's Government's policy contemplates concession to Great Britain of

Mandate for Palestine. Terms of Mandate will embody substance of declaration of November 2, 1917. Arabs will not be despoiled of their land nor required to leave the country. There is no question of majority being subjected to the rule of minority, nor does Zionist programme contemplate this.' Echoing the memorandum which Samuel and Weizmann had submitted, the Arabs were to be told that the establishment of a Jewish National Home was a *chose jugee* and continued agitation would be useless and detrimental.[43]

> 'And Zionism, be it right or wrong, good or bad, is rooted in age-long traditions, in present needs, in future hopes, of far profounder import than the desires and prejudices of the 700,000 Arabs who now inhabit that ancient land'.
> **MEMORANDUM BY BALFOUR, 11 AUGUST 1919**

On 11 August, Balfour felt compelled to pen a major analysis on the affairs of Syria, Palestine and Mesopotamia. Palestine was not really its main focus, since what was clearly exercising him were the continuing Anglo-French differences over Syria. Even so, what he had to say about Palestine reveals a great deal about his true feelings towards Zionism and the Arabs. Conceding that there was no intention of even going through the motions of consulting the wishes of the inhabitants, he wrote: 'The four Great Powers are committed to Zionism. And Zionism, be it right or wrong, good or bad, is rooted in age-long traditions, in present needs, in future hopes, of far profounder import than the desires and prejudices of the 700,000 Arabs who now inhabit that ancient land.' The Powers, he concluded, had made 'no declaration of policy which, at least in the letter, they have not always intended to violate'.[44]

That autumn, the Weizmanns travelled to Palestine. It was

Vera Weizmann's first visit, and it proved to be a sore disappointment after the anticipation she had felt. In particular, the trained doctor in her was appalled by what the pioneering Jewish women were doing. Their physical labour, she felt, was undermining both their health and their prospects for future motherhood. In building up the National Home, they were sacrificing their homes and diet. Before leaving for England, she sent them some flowers to thank them for their hospitality.[45]

Weizmann as President of Israel during a visit to President Truman in Washington, 29 May 1948.

III

The Legacy

5

San Remo, the National Home and Arab resistance

The Treaty of Versailles came into force on 10 January 1920, even though on 19 November 1919, the American Senate had failed to ratify it. While the Treaty set the complex terms of the peace settlement with Germany, important issues remained to be resolved, not least in the Middle East. In the light of the forthcoming conference at San Remo in Italy, which would at last move forward the peace settlement with Turkey, Weizmann sought to reinforce his message with Robert Vansittart of the Foreign Office. He was concerned to drive home that Palestine's position as the Jewish National Home should be embodied in the peace treaty with Turkey. What was perturbing him, it seems, was the possible nature of the Mandate system. The Mandates for the other areas of the former Turkish empire were to be administered in the interests of their inhabitants, while the overriding purpose of that for Palestine, as far as the Zionists were concerned, was to be the creation of the Jewish National Home, the rights of the inhabitants being safeguarded.[1] He need not have worried, as it happened, but before the conference took place he was to have an experience which gave him even more reason to worry about the future.

What Weizmann encountered at first hand was the growing strength of Arab opposition to the Jewish presence in Palestine, which he had been aware of for some time. In March 1920, he made a return visit to the country in the company of his elder son. The timing was bad, since the anger of the Arab population had been rising on a number of counts. There was growing frustration that promises they believed had been made over Arab independence were not being honoured. There was fear that the Balfour Declaration would lead to Arab subordination to the Jews as a consequence of massive Jewish immigration. Finally, there were hopes of an Arab state embracing both Syria and Palestine, ruled by Feisal from Damascus.[2] During his temporary stopover in Egypt, Weizmann became aware of growing unrest in parts of Palestine, which had resulted in the death of, amongst others, Joseph Trumpeldor, who had been organising Jewish defence groups. On 25 March, Weizmann summed up his impressions of the current situation in Palestine in a deeply pessimistic letter to the Zionist Executive in London. In this he castigated the military authorities for what he believed was their open hostility to the Jews and partiality towards the Arabs. The prevailing view amongst the officers, he reported, was that the Balfour Declaration had been a mistake. Such British attitudes were encouraging the Arabs, and, he confided, he had lost faith in Feisal.[3]

What then happened was tragic, but also a grim portent of what was to come in the affairs of Palestine. The proclamation of Feisal as King of Syria on 8 March 1920 by a Syrian Congress in which Palestinians were represented stirred demonstrations of support in various parts of Palestine, leading the British to ban further such events. Nevertheless, such a demonstration did take place in Jerusalem on 4 April on the occasion of the Muslim festival of Nabi Musa, which coincided with the Christian Easter and Jewish Passover. Amongst the organisers were the Mayor of Jerusalem, Musa Kasim al-Husayni, the newspaper editor Arif al-Arif and the young man who was soon to become the *bête noire* of both the Jews and the British, Haj Amin al-Husayni. Both Husaynis belonged to Jerusalem's most prominent Arab family. Once again, support for Feisal was the focus of the demonstration. In the violence which then followed, five Jews were killed and over 200 wounded, while four Arabs were killed and 21 wounded.[4] Weizmann, who had gone to Haifa to celebrate Passover with his mother, who had settled in Palestine after the Russian Revolution, returned with his son to Jerusalem to find the city under military occupation. Although he had been out of the city when the violence had broken out, there is no doubt that what had happened deeply shocked Weizmann, for whom these events were all too reminiscent of the Russian pogroms, only this time under the British.[5] Apart from what it revealed about Arab hostility, the outbreak also exposed the limitations of British power, which was far from reassuring to the Jews. Weizmann was fiercely critical of the actions of the British forces in disarming Jews. It was also alarming to the Jews that while Arif al-Arif and Amin al-Husayni were given 10-year sentences *in absentia*, Vladimir Jabotinsky, who had sought to mobilise young Jews, was sentenced to 15 years. However, what deeply worried Weizmann was the possible impact of these events on the deliberations and decisions of the forthcoming San Remo conference.[6]

It was, therefore, a rather disheartened, apprehensive, and by his own account somewhat grimy Weizmann who travelled from Palestine to San Remo. Since the conference lasted from 18 to 26 April and the future of Palestine was one of the last items under discussion, he did not have much to do. It was, perhaps, a measure of the toll that recent events had taken that in the course of his train journey to San Remo, he confided in Vera his distrust of the British.[7] Once there, however, several things occurred which relieved his anxieties. Balfour was able to reassure him that he and Curzon were agreed that the recent events in Jerusalem would not affect British policy, which had been Weizmann's main concern. He also learned that Lloyd George and Balfour were agreed that Samuel should be the first British High Commissioner in Palestine.

The future of Palestine came before the Supreme Council on 24 April, chaired by the Italian premier Francesco Nitti. Lloyd George, Curzon and Robert Vansittart were present for Britain, Prime Minister Alexandre Millerand and Philippe Berthelot of the Ministry of Foreign Affairs represented France, and Mr Matsui spoke for Japan. They were joined by the American Ambassador to Italy, Robert Underwood Johnson. Curzon opened by referring to the Balfour Declaration, which he grandly, if somewhat inaccurately, claimed had promised Palestine as the National Home of the Jews of the world, and which he said had been accepted by the major powers. What he wanted was that the Declaration as it stood should be incorporated into the treaty, claiming that he had resisted attempts by the Zionists to have its terms expanded. Curzon had clearly got wind of the fact that the French were still having reservations. A lengthy debate with Berthelot confirmed this to be the case.

Berthelot countered by questioning several of Curzon's assertions. There had not, he stated, been any official acceptance of the Balfour Declaration by the Allied governments.

While the French did not wish to thwart Britain's desire to give the Jews a National Home in Palestine, he queried what this meant. If it were to be different to other states, then it would create difficulties in the Muslim and Christian world. He was clearly thinking of France's large stake in Muslim North Africa, as well as her plans for Syria. The Christian dimension would emerge in the course of the ensuing debate. It would be best, he said, to refer the matter to the League of Nations. Curzon then treated Berthelot to a brief history lesson. He was not quite accurate in saying that Balfour had issued the Declaration on behalf of the Zionists, he said, but then went on to claim that it had been accepted by Pichon, then Head of the French Foreign Office, by President Wilson, and by the governments of Greece, China, Serbia and Siam. The two men then wrangled for some time over exactly what Pichon had, or had not, agreed to.

Millerand adopted a rather softer line, while Nitti tried to bring the two sides to an understanding. Berthelot eagerly pounced on a statement by Matsui that his government had never accepted the Declaration, as confirmation of his point that it was not official Allied policy. It then emerged that what was really troubling the French, and to an extent Nitti, was the position of the Catholic community in Palestine. The Vatican had made public its view that the French, and not the British, should be the protector of Catholic interests in the country. Lloyd George was adamant that there could not be two mandatory powers in Palestine. The French were also keen to assert the political, as opposed to the civil and religious, rights of the non-Jewish communities of Palestine, which had been expressed in the Balfour Declaration, but Millerand conceded that he would be satisfied if this were placed on record.[8]

The following day, the conference returned to the question of Mandates, especially the question of boundaries. There was no repetition of the prolonged wrangling of the previous day. The border of Palestine was linked to that of the Mosul region, which had been a point of contention between Britain and France. The main issue between them was where the northern border of Palestine was to lie. The Zionist hope was that it would be along the Litani River, which would include the headwaters of the River Jordan. While acknowledging their case, Lloyd George was prepared to concede that this area had never formed part of Palestine, and that, as a result, the border should be focused on the town of Dan. On hearing this concession, Berthelot asked whether the conference could now decide that the Mandates for Mesopotamia, or Iraq as it was to be known after 1921, and Palestine should be given to Britain, and Syria to France. Nitti agreed. The formal agreement regarding Palestine was that the country's administration be entrusted to a Mandatory to be chosen by the Principal Allied Powers. The chosen Mandatory power was Britain. The Mandatory was charged with putting into effect the Declaration of November 1917, and it was confirmed that this had been adopted by the other Allies.[9]

As the conference ended, Lloyd George emerged to inform Weizmann of the decision to award the Palestine Mandate to Britain, with the incorporation of the Balfour Declaration as an essential proviso. He was also told that Samuel would be appointed High Commissioner, and that there would be changes in the Palestine administration. In Weizmann's view the outcome was of equal significance to the Balfour Declaration, and in his letter to Vera telling her of what had been agreed he heralded it as the dawn of a new Palestine.[10] With a British Mandate based upon the Balfour Declaration now in his pocket, Weizmann's stature within the Zionist movement was unique and unassailable, or so it seemed.

In fact, the International Zionist Conference, the first truly representative Zionist congress since 1913, which was held in London in early July 1920, proved to be far from harmonious. Weizmann's address opened with what can only be described as a paean of praise for the British leaders, Balfour and Lloyd George, of course, but also Curzon for the way in which he had defended the Zionist position at San Remo. He reminded his audience that the conditions for creating the National Home had been established, and that a sympathiser, Samuel, had been given responsibility for Palestine. If they were to make Palestine as Jewish a country as quickly as possible, then the work had to be set in hand over the next few years. Not to do so would raise a question mark against the Zionist enterprise. His hope was to settle some 30,000 to 50,000 Jews in the first year. Such a level of immigration would require land purchases which did not infringe the rights of the Arabs. A major objective, he argued, was to secure the goodwill of the Palestinian Arabs; failure to do this would poison their efforts. Echoing his earlier contacts with Feisal, he argued that Jewish expertise could assist with the development of the Arab world. In his peroration he returned to the theme that the conditions for the re-creation of the Jewish nation had been secured. It was now up to the Jews themselves to achieve it.[11]

Despite his fine oratory and recent triumph, the Conference was a far from happy experience for Weizmann, who found himself criticised by, amongst others, Ben-Gurion, who now made his debut in the world of international Zionism. Ben-Gurion's power base was starkly different to that of Weizmann; namely, the *Achdut ha-Avodah*, the Socialist-Zionist

Turkey and the Near East 1923

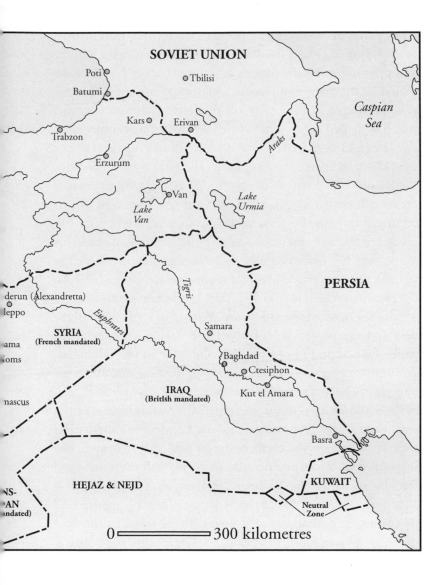

Association of Workers of Palestine, which had been formed in the spring of 1919. His attack on Weizmann was both bitter and personal, accusing him of creating a barrier between the administration and the Jews of Palestine. Moreover, his concessions had led to hostility on the part of the government that had helped incite Arab violence. Finally, he claimed that the Jews had been better served under the Turks than under the British, a curious notion given the Balfour Declaration. Weizmann had little difficulty in rebutting this intemperate assault on his leadership, but it did not bode well for his relationship with the Jews of Palestine, who were, after all, pivotal to the movement's success. Ben-Gurion had made his mark, and his influence was to grow significantly with the years. It was an inauspicious start to a relationship between the two men which would ultimately end on a bitter note.[12]

More serious at the time was Weizmann's rift with Brandeis and the leadership of the large American contingent which had come to London. With his base in the Olympian atmosphere of the Supreme Court in Washington, Brandeis had always been a somewhat improbable Zionist leader, and his punctilious legal mind was repelled by what he saw of the somewhat scatty preparations for the London conference. At root, however, was a clash between how the two men saw the future of Zionism. Brandeis and his followers believed that by securing the Balfour Declaration and the British Mandate, Zionism had achieved its political purpose and objectives, and hence should now turn its hand to the economic development of Palestine. For Weizmann, the political struggle was only just beginning. Brandeis's proposal that the Zionist organisation should focus on economic activity was clearly defeated on the floor of the conference. But Brandeis believed, seemingly with justice, that Weizmann had lobbied against his ideas for a reorganisation of the Zionist leadership, and the two leaders also quarrelled over the size of the American contribution to the budget. The breach between these two gifted men was never to be repaired. The conference concluded with Brandeis's appointment as Honorary President of the World Zionist Organisation, with Weizmann as its President. At last, Weizmann had a position of strength from which he could operate, but it had been purchased at a price, both in Palestine and the United States.[13]

When Sir Herbert Samuel, as he had become, assumed office as High Commissioner and Commander-in-Chief in Palestine on 30 June 1920 it seemed to herald the fulfilment of Zionist dreams. Not only was his one of the main voices which had led to the Balfour Declaration, but after nearly two millennia a Jew stood at the head of Palestine's affairs. But it was not as simple as that. The achievement of the Zionist dream, at least as it had evolved under Weizmann, rested on two external conditions; sustained British commitment to the idea of a National Home and Arab, especially Palestinian Arab, acquiescence in it. Samuel's arrival in Palestine was not reassuring on either count. His journey from Jaffa to Jerusalem had to be changed to take account of rumours of plots on his life, and he had to be given an escort of armoured cars for his journey from the Jerusalem railway station to the government house on the Mount of Olives, where the outgoing Chief Administrator,

> In his memoirs, Samuel recounts his arrival at his headquarters on the Mount of Olives, where he was greeted by the outgoing Chief Administrator, Major-General Sir Louis Bols. To Samuel's evident bemusement the General asked him to sign a receipt, and when asked what it was for, Bols replied that it was for Palestine. Bols then produced a typewritten receipt for the country, 'One Palestine, Complete', which Samuel duly signed. According to Samuel, Bols subsequently kept this document framed in his office.

Major-General Sir Louis Bols, persuaded him to sign a receipt for Palestine. It was hardly a triumphal entry, though he did receive a 17-gun salute.[14]

The Easter 1920 disturbances in Jerusalem which had so shocked Weizmann were by no means unique to Palestine, although they obviously reflected local concerns. In January 1919, the murder of two unarmed members of the Royal Irish Constabulary in County Tipperary ushered in the struggle which was to result in the partition of Ireland and the emergence of the Irish Free State in 1922. In the spring of 1919, the Punjab disturbances in India climaxed in the infamous Jallianwala Bagh massacre at Amritsar on 13 April when 379 unarmed Indians were shot dead. At the end of 1920, Mahatma Gandhi began his campaign of non-violent resistance to bring British rule in India to an end. Allied with him was the Khilafat movement, which mobilised Indian Muslims on the issue of the Turkish Caliphate. But the Middle East, too, was restive under the new systems which the victorious Allies seemed set on imposing. In March 1919, rebellion broke out in Egypt, and although it was quickly suppressed by British troops, the Egyptians never rested easily under the British Protectorate, which formally ended in 1922 even though British imperial interests remained paramount. The assassination of Sir Lee Stack, Governor-General of the Sudan and Sirdar of the Egyptian army, in the centre of Cairo in 1924 was symptomatic of the mood in the country.

The situation in Iraq was even more volatile. The award of the Mandate to Britain at the San Remo Conference was followed by a widespread revolt which broke out in July 1920. The reasons for this outbreak were a matter of some controversy at the time. The Acting Civil Commissioner, the gifted but imperious Arnold T Wilson, viewed what happened in part as the result of incitement from Feisal's government in Damascus, although even he could not disguise the fact of opposition to the Mandate. In fairness to Wilson, he was doubtful whether the Shi'a Arabs or the Kurds could come to terms with a government dominated by Sunni Arabs, the issue which has been at the heart of the country's problems ever since.[15] T E Lawrence, on the other hand, put the matter with stark simplicity in a letter published in *The Times* on 23 July. The Arabs, he pointed out, had not fought the Turks simply to change masters, but for their independence. The insurrection, which lasted into 1921, claimed an estimated 8,450 Iraqi lives. It was a severe strain on the British and Indian armies, overstretched as they were. At the outbreak of the rebellion, there were 9,800 British and 25,000 Indian soldiers, but over the summer of 1920 a further 20 battalions had to be sent from India. British and Indian army casualties were 426 killed, 1,228 wounded, and 615 missing or prisoners. The Mandate for Iraq was proving a poisoned chalice.[16]

Just as the British Mandate was being challenged in Iraq, the French were relentlessly imposing theirs over Syria, at the expense of Britain's old ally Feisal. In November 1919, the British army evacuated Syria, leaving the way open for a French military occupation. The newly-appointed High Commissioner for Syria and Lebanon, General Henri Gouraud, was determined to assert French control, and, with some 80,000 troops equipped with tanks, artillery and aircraft, he had ample military force with which to do it. On 14 July 1920, Gouraud presented Feisal with an ultimatum, the essence of which was acceptance of the French Mandate. Conscious of his weakness, Feisal accepted Gouraud's terms, but as the French forces continued to close in on Damascus and Aleppo popular disturbances broke out in protest. On 25

July, the French entered Damascus, and Feisal was forced to leave his fledgling kingdom.[17] Feisal's expulsion was a further blow to the Palestinian Arabs, who were still reeling from the San Remo decisions. Not only was it a humiliation, but it set at naught the assurances Feisal had given Weizmann, as he had said it would. In the event, Feisal was offered some consolation by the British. Shaken by the scale of events in Iraq, in October 1920 Sir Percy Cox, who had replaced Wilson, established a Council of State in Baghdad. The events of 1920 were an inauspicious beginning for the new British *imperium* in the Middle East on which the Zionists, and Weizmann in particular, had based their hopes.

The issue of Iraq, or more exactly the costs Britain was having to sustain there, was addressed by the newly appointed Colonial Secretary, Winston Churchill, at the Cairo Conference in March 1921. Churchill's tenure of the office, though relatively brief, was to have a far-reaching impact on the way in which the British were to define the National Home. The basis of Churchill's solution for Iraq was that the throne should be offered to Feisal. In July 1921, the Council of State in Baghdad duly obliged, and Feisal was crowned on 23 August, beginning a new phase in the country's history, which the following year saw the draft Mandate replaced by a Treaty of Alliance between Iraq and Britain. Of more direct relevance to the future of Palestine was that Transjordan, which the Zionists had assumed to be part of the Mandate for Palestine, was entrusted to Feisal's brother Abdullah. When the Cairo Conference ended, Churchill travelled to Jerusalem to discuss the future of Transjordan with Abdullah.[18]

While in Jerusalem, Churchill addressed Arab and Zionist delegations on 30 March 1921. The Palestinians had already submitted a memorandum asking him to repudiate the Balfour

Declaration and halt immigration. He made it clear to them that he had no intention of doing either. But of particular significance for the future was what he went on to say about the Balfour Declaration. Emphasising that Balfour had used the term *a* National Home rather than *the* National Home, he said that this did not mean a Jewish government which would dominate the Arabs. More ominously, from a Zionist perspective, he used the term 'national centre' when talking about the National Home, a term which was soon to take on some significance. Interestingly, this qualification did not feature in his response to the Zionist delegation. Rather he confirmed the British government's commitment to the Balfour Declaration, while emphasising this had to be undertaken without prejudice to the country's existing majority. He also warned them that the Arabs were very much afraid for their future. Just exactly how the Arabs felt would soon be revealed.[19]

While these events were unfolding in the Middle East, Weizmann briefly returned to Palestine prior to making his first visit to the United States in April 1921; the ostensible purpose was to stimulate interest in Hebrew University, still a barren site on Mount Scopus, and to establish the Palestine Foundation Fund, the *Keren Hayesod*, in the country. Behind this journey, of course, lay his simmering feud with Brandeis and his supporters in the American Zionist movement, which had come into sharper focus at the annual congress of the Zionist Organization of America (ZOA) in November 1920. Here Brandeis's supporters effectively downgraded the *Keren Hayesod*. Although he was, in a sense, entering the lions' den, Weizmann had brought with him a strong delegation, including Ussishkin, had enlisted the active support of Albert Einstein, and was welcomed on his arrival in the city by a ecstatic crowd of New York Jews.

It was not long before he locked horns with the ZOA's leadership. Even before he had disembarked, he was met by Judge Julian Mack, President of the ZOA, who had handed him a memorandum setting out the views of Brandeis and his supporters. What it proposed amounted, in Weizmann's view, to nothing less than a disaggregation of the Zionist movement into its component parts. For his part, Weizmann was clear that a united Zionism was of the essence, and, as a result, he could not accept the terms of the memorandum. In doing so, he was openly confronting the established leadership of the ZOA, Brandeis, Mack, Felix Frankfurter, Robert Szold, Jacob de Haas and Stephen Wise, as eminent a group of American Jews as could be imagined. In contrast, Weizmann's American supporters, like Louis Lipsky, seemed lesser figures. But Weizmann's instincts told him that the sentiments of American Jewry were with him, and Ussishkin shared his view that they should not surrender to the American leadership.

Even so, attempts at a compromise were made, but proved inconclusive. By the end of April, Brandeis was writing to his wife and to Frankfurter in bitter terms of Weizmann, whom he had evidently come to detest. For his part, Weizmann issued a statement as President of the World Zionist Organisation establishing the *Keren Hayesod* in the United States. This action brought the fraught relations between the two groups to a head, the confrontation coming at the 24th Annual Convention of the ZOA which met in the city of Cleveland from 5–8 June 1921. Weizmann and his delegation attended, but did not speak, although the deliberations and votes went decisively in their favour. Brandeis and Mack had been in contact prior to the Convention about their positions should the decisions go against them, and they promptly resigned their offices together with their main supporters.

On 19 June, Brandeis formally tendered his resignation as Honorary President of the World Zionist Organisation. Weizmann and his supporters within American Zionism were left in possession of the field, but at the cost of a bitter rift in the leadership of one of the world's most vibrant Jewish communities, the echoes of which would be heard for years to come.[20]

But just as Weizmann was consolidating his grip on the Zionist movement, Churchill's warning about Arab fears was realised to an extent that put the outbreak of violence in 1920 into the shade. When Samuel had been in office just a week, he proclaimed an amnesty for those who had been involved in the spring disturbances, which included Jabotinsky, for whose release Weizmann had been vigorously campaigning. In August 1920, this amnesty was extended to the two principal Arab fugitives, Arif al-Arif and Amin al-Husayni, thus opening the way for the latter's entry into active Palestinian politics. His opportunity came in March 1921 with the death of the Grand Mufti of Jerusalem, his half-brother Kamil al-Husayni. Amin immediately campaigned to succeed him, apparently assuring the British of his good offices. Before this could happen, however, trouble broke out in a way that could hardly have been expected. On May Day, a quarrel occurred between communist and non-communist Jews in Jaffa, which, for reasons that are not entirely clear, sparked an Arab attack on the city's Jewish population, and then on five Jewish settlements. In the resulting violence, 47 Jews were killed and 146 wounded, while the police and troops killed 48 Arabs and wounded 73 others. In the aftermath, Amin al-Husayni was confirmed as Mufti, an appointment which saw him develop into one of Zionism's deadliest enemies.[21]

While the Mufti's activism lay in the future, more serious

from the perspective of Weizmann and the Zionists was both the scale of the violence and what it revealed about the state of Arab opinion. The official enquiry into what happened, chaired by the Chief Justice of Palestine, Sir Thomas Haycraft, left little doubt as to the latter. It identified the principal cause as hostility towards the Jews, linked to Jewish immigration and Arab perceptions of Zionist policies. Dismissing as superficial Zionist claims that the violence had really been directed against British rule, Haycraft identified the basic cause as the Arab fear that the increasing Jewish immigration would result in the loss of their economic and political position. He further pointed to the lifestyle of the young Jewish immigrants which jarred with the Arab way of life. Hostility to the Jews also cut across class barriers and the Muslim-Christian divide. By any reckoning, it was a sober analysis for the British and a disturbing one for the Zionists.[22]

Samuel now turned to appease the Arabs. One of his first decisions following the outbreak of violence was to suspend immigration, an action which caused understandable consternation among the Jews. While he intended this to be temporary, Samuel indicated to Churchill that it should only be resumed if there were projects ready for the new immigrants. Part of his proposed solution was to create representative institutions through enlarging his Advisory Council with elected Muslim, Jewish and Christian members. He also confided in Churchill that the Zionist leaders had to recognise that their policies would not be possible in the face of the opposition of the greater part of the Palestinian population.[23] The high hopes that Weizmann and the Zionists had placed in him at the time of the San Remo Conference were now turning sour. The appointment as Mufti of Haj Amin, whom they identified with the Jerusalem riots of the previous year, was distinctly unwelcome.[24] The changing tone of British policy, already signalled in Samuel's letter to Churchill, could be clearly seen in his royal birthday speech in Jerusalem on 3 June 1921, in which he denied that Britain would countenance a Jewish government over the non-Jewish majority. He also introduced the concept of economic absorbability, which, he claimed, should govern immigration policy, and announced that the government was considering a partially elected legislative council. Even before the Mandate had been formally endorsed by the League, qualifications on the Balfour Declaration were beginning to emerge. Given the fact that Churchill had been closely consulted on Samuel's speech, Weizmann was spurred into action.[25]

Clearly alarmed by its content and tone, Weizmann attended a meeting at Balfour's house, during which he confided his fears in Lloyd George, Churchill and Maurice Hankey. That he had such access to the Prime Minister and Colonial Secretary was a clear answer to his critics in the Zionist movement, since neither Brandeis nor Ben-Gurion could have brought together such key figures at that time. After discussing his visit to the United States, Weizmann cut quickly to the point, castigating Samuel's speech as a negation of the Balfour Declaration. Challenged on the point by Churchill, he then compared the two documents, claiming that the speech would prevent the creation of a Jewish majority, which the Declaration had sanctioned. At this point Lloyd George and Balfour both interjected, reassuring Weizmann that the Declaration had anticipated an eventual Jewish state. Turning to the defence of the Jews, Weizmann apparently secured covert approval for bringing weapons into Palestine. He then turned to the legislative council proposal. While Churchill argued that this was being undertaken in Iraq and

Transjordan, Weizmann responded, with some justice, that it was only being proposed for Palestine because the British had been forced into it. Lloyd George, Churchill and Balfour were inclined to agree. Weizmann then came to what was clearly his main concern; namely, that to set up representative government would mean abandoning Palestine, at which point Lloyd George told Churchill that the country must not be given representative government. The Colonial Secretary responded that he might have to bring the idea to the Cabinet, but that the Jewish National Home would be excluded from it. Weizmann denied that such a thing was possible.[26]

Impressive though his intervention in London was, it could not in itself halt the Arab offensive against Zionist aims. In May 1921, the Palestine Arab Congress resolved to send a joint Muslim-Christian delegation, headed by Musa Kasim al-Husayni and Shibly al-Jamal, to Rome, where they were received by the Pope. The delegation then travelled to Paris, Geneva and London to lobby against the Balfour Declaration's incorporation into the proposed Mandate. In anticipation of their visit, Churchill felt the need to present his appreciation of the situation in Palestine to the Cabinet. His analysis was that the country was in ferment, with the Zionists' policies unpopular with everyone except themselves. He reported that elective institutions had been refused in deference to the Zionists, and that, as a result, the Arabs contrasted their situation with that of Iraq. Nevertheless, Churchill said that if it were the wish of the Cabinet, he would implement the Balfour Declaration and the San Remo decisions. Reinforcing its chief's views, the Colonial Office advised that the Arabs objected to Zionist policy *per se*, and that, as a result, its aims could only be achieved by showing that Jewish immigration would not undermine their existing position. The tactic to be followed should be that of allowing gradual Jewish immigration linked to the ability of the country to absorb it.[27]

The Palestinian delegation was in London for almost a year, in the course of which it became clear that the British would not accede to their demands that they renounce the Balfour Declaration, end Jewish immigration, and grant self-government. A meeting with Weizmann, arranged by Churchill, was fruitless.[28] Churchill's advice to the Cabinet was that there were two choices. It could revoke the Balfour Declaration, refer the Mandate to the League of Nations, set up an Arab government, and curtail or stop Jewish immigration. Alternatively, it could pursue existing policy and arm the Jews. A draft announcement by Weizmann to that effect failed to find support, however. This was an unpalatable choice, and it is hardly surprising that the ministers failed to make it. Discussion centred around two issues; namely, the fact that Britain had made a pledge in the Balfour Declaration, and the growing power of the Arabs in the territories around Palestine. While some argued that the Arabs had no right to Palestine since they had not developed it, others pointed to the inconsistency in the Balfour Declaration in promising support for a National Home while respecting the rights of the Arabs.[29]

For his part, Samuel was increasingly worried by the situation in Palestine, especially given the pressure he was under to reduce the costs of its garrison. On 14 October 1921, he wrote to Churchill expressing his fears of the repercussions should the Arab delegation to London return dissatisfied. In the first instance, he pressed for the ratification of the Mandate, the delay in which he identified as contributing to his political, economic and financial difficulties. Secondly, he turned to the critical question of Arab-Jewish relations. What he was concerned to drive home was his belief that many Arabs would be prepared to accept the definition of the National Home which he had set out in his speech of 3 June, as long as this was held to be British policy. Again, however, he turned to Weizmann's Peace Conference statement that Palestine would become as Jewish as England is English, which, he said, was repeatedly quoted in the press in Palestine, as being inconsistent with the idea that Arabs and Jews could work for a common future. Samuel concluded by saying that the Arabs should stop asking for the abrogation of the Balfour Declaration, but also that, for their part, the Zionists should acknowledge that they were aiming to build a democratic commonwealth rather than a state in which they would be politically privileged, and that the statement about Palestine becoming as Jewish as England is English be amended to take into account that Palestine was a common home.[30]

Samuel's letter was poorly timed, since three days earlier negotiations for an Irish settlement had got under way in London, with Churchill as a key member of the British team. Compared with Ireland, Palestine was a peripheral British interest. Even after the treaty was signed on 6 December 1921, Churchill's involvement in Irish affairs increased since as a Dominion the emergent Irish Free State came under his portfolio as Colonial Secretary. When Sinn Fein split on 7 January 1922 between the supporters of Arthur Griffith and Michael Collins, who had signed the treaty, and those of Eamon de Valera, who rejected it, Irish affairs once again took on a dangerous dimension. With anti-Catholic pogroms in Belfast in the spring of 1922 and the outbreak of civil war in the Free State on 28 June, Ireland was never far from Churchill's mind. He was also engaged in a simmering, but increasingly acrimonious, dispute with Edwin Montagu over the rights of the

Indian community in Kenya. While it would be going too far to say that Palestine was a distraction, its problems needed to be addressed.

If the purpose of the Arab delegation had been to seek a reversal of government policy, then they had clearly failed. What they had succeeded in doing was driving home that the Arabs of Palestine were adamantly opposed to British policies, something confirmed in November 1921 with the publication of the Haycraft committee inquiry into the May disturbances. The measure of their success may be seen in a mounting campaign against the Balfour Declaration in sections of the British press, including those owned by the powerful newspaper barons, Lords Northcliffe and Beaverbrook. Once again trying to square the circle, on 11 April 1922 John Shuckburgh wrote to the delegation on Churchill's behalf confirming that there would be no retreat from the Balfour Declaration, but that the government's purpose was to ensure that the section of the Declaration referring to the position of the non-Jewish inhabitants was carried out.[31]

With ratification of the Mandate now imminent, confirming this became the purpose of British policy, and in May Samuel came to London to assist in reaching a formula which would achieve it. Weizmann, meanwhile, allowed himself to be diverted into visiting Rome, where he believed the Vatican was a key opponent of the Balfour Declaration, as well as Berlin and Paris. On his return, he had to confront the uncomfortable fact that the House of Lords had voted to repeal the Balfour Declaration, although fortunately for the Zionists the House of Commons rejected a similar motion. While Balfour reassured Weizmann that the House of Lords vote was immaterial, it was yet another indication that British support could not necessarily be taken for granted.[32] It stands repeating that this was a time when Irish affairs were consuming Churchill's attention with the seizure of the Pettigo-Belleek Triangle in County Fermanagh in Northern Ireland by Republican forces, and that Conservative support for the Lloyd George coalition was fast eroding, of which the House of Lords vote on the Balfour Declaration was a clear symptom, whatever its author might say.

This highly febrile political situation saw the publication, on 3 June 1922, of the *Statement of British Policy in Palestine*, commonly referred to as the Churchill White Paper. Here Weizmann's response to Lansing came back to bite him. 'Unauthorised statements' it said, 'have been made to the effect that the purpose in view is to create a wholly Jewish Palestine. Phrases have been used such as that Palestine is to become "as Jewish as England is English.". His Majesty's Government regard any such expectation as impracticable and have no such aim in view'. Referring to the fears which the Arab delegation had expressed, the *Statement* denied that there had ever been any intention of subordinating the Arabs, pointing out that the Balfour Declaration had made it clear that the National Home was to be founded 'in Palestine' rather than being the whole of the country. Addressing the Zionists, it confirmed that the Balfour Declaration was not up for negotiation, affirming the 'ancient historic connection' of the Jews to the National Home and that they were in Palestine 'as of right and not on sufferance'. It was the definition of the National Home that was problematic for Weizmann and the Zionists, however: 'When it is asked what is meant by the development of the Jewish National Home in Palestine, it may be answered that it is not the imposition of a Jewish nationality upon the inhabitants of Palestine as a whole, but the further development of the existing Jewish community, with the assistance of Jews in other parts of the world, in order that it may become a centre in which the Jewish people as a whole may take, on grounds of religion and race, an interest and a pride.' Two other elements displeased and alarmed the Zionists. The first was the acceptance of the establishment of a legislative council, albeit gradually, which the Arabs had been demanding, but which the Zionists had opposed and which Weizmann had been given reason to believe Lloyd George had ruled out. The other was confirmation of the principle that immigration into Palestine should be dependant on its absorptive capacity, an unwelcome concept introduced by Samuel in his 3 July speech the previous year. To the Zionists it was a negation of their conviction that only through immigration could the economy of the National Home be developed.[33]

> 'Phrases have been used such as that Palestine is to become "as Jewish as England is English." His Majesty's Government regard any such expectation as impracticable and have no such aim in view.'
> **CHURCHILL WHITE PAPER, 1922**

Weizmann rightly regarded the terms of the announcement as a considerable retreat from the Balfour Declaration, but since he had been told that confirmation of the Mandate depended on Jewish acceptance of the White Paper, he had been left with no alternative but to do so. He was even prepared to argue that the idea of economic absorbability could work to the Jews' advantage, though he later had to confess that this had not been the case. Even so, on 18 June 1922, Weizmann wrote on behalf of the Zionist Organisation, confirming acceptance of the new policy as set out in the *Statement*. The previous day, the Arabs had rejected it, as they were to do with so many initiatives in the future, usually to their disadvantage, as it turned out.[34]

The way was now open for the Council of the League of Nations to confirm unanimously the Mandate on 24 July 1922. Weizmann's fear that the predominantly Catholic countries of Spain and Brazil would demur proved to be unfounded, and an attempt by the Papal Nuncio to defer the item was thwarted by the French.[35] In many respects, the terms of the Mandate were what the Zionists had been working to secure and the Arabs had hoped to prevent. Crucially, the Preamble formally incorporated the Balfour Declaration into the Mandate, and, in a sense, went even further by recognising 'the historical connection of the Jewish people with Palestine and to the grounds for reconstituting their National Home in the country'. Under Article 2 of the Mandate, Britain was to place Palestine 'under such political, administrative and economic conditions as will secure the establishment of the Jewish National Home, as laid down in the preamble, and the development of self-governing institutions, and also for safeguarding the civil and religious rights of all the inhabitants of Palestine, irrespective of race and religion'. Articles 4 and 6 of the Mandate sanctioned the creation of a Jewish Agency, and charged the Mandatory with facilitating Jewish immigration, while making sure that the rights and position of others were not prejudiced. Finally, Article 25 permitted the Mandatory to make separate provision for the land to the east of the river Jordan, which was confirmed by the League on 16 September.[36] The campaign to secure the British Mandate for Palestine, which would include the implementation of the Balfour Declaration, was one which Weizmann had waged for five gruelling years. Now, at last, this key objective had been secured, but in the meantime events in Palestine had been gathering pace.

6

Weizmann: the prisoner of Zion?

With the coming into effect of the Mandate, Weizmann's political career entered a new phase. Now a man in middle age and a respected scientist, the patents from his scientific work and shrewd investments enabled him to lead a prosperous upper middle-class life in London. It was not always a happy one, however. His work for the Zionist movement necessarily involved long absences from home, and in the mid-1920s his marriage apparently went through a troubled period. Both his sons were to reject his Zionism.[1] He was the acknowledged, if not always unchallenged, leader of Zionism. His diplomatic skills were undimmed, but the men who had responded so positively to his arguments were passing from the scene. Sykes, of course, was already dead, and Feisal was not the leader of the Arab national movement as he and Weizmann had hoped he would become. Perhaps the greatest loss was Lloyd George, who had displayed an almost emotional attachment to Zionism. His coalition government fell apart in October 1922, and, despite his consummate talents, he never again held office. His successors as Prime Minister, Andrew Bonar Law, Stanley Baldwin, Ramsay MacDonald and Neville Chamberlain were men who had other priorities. Balfour and Curzon were spent forces in British politics, while Samuel, doggedly loyal to the ailing Liberal Party, only briefly returned to office as Home Secretary in 1931–2. Churchill pursued an erratic political course, despite a period as Chancellor of the Exchequer, until his great moment came in May 1940.

The prospects for Zionism now rested, above all, on how the National Home fared in Palestine. In 1922, the British estimated the population at 589,000 Muslims, 83,000 Jews and 71,000 Christians, who were mostly Arabs. By 1925, when Samuel's period as High Commissioner came to an end, the Jewish population had grown to 108,000, but this proved to be a boom year as far as immigration was concerned. That year some 33,801 Jews came into Palestine, while 2,151 left. Economic conditions in the country were far from easy, and in 1927 there were only 2,713 Jewish immigrants, whereas 5,071 left the country.[2] Even so, the National Home was beginning to make progress. By 1929, the population of Tel Aviv had grown to 46,000, and it was acquiring critical mass as a Jewish city.[3] Much of the organisation of the Jewish community turned on the powerful trade union movement, the *Histadrut*, or General Federation of Jewish Labour, which had been formed in 1920. Elected to its council in November 1921, Ben-Gurion became its driving force, rapidly emerging as the dominant personality in the *Yishuv*, as the Jewish community in Palestine was called. As his stature grew, it became evident that in time he would come to rival Weizmann.[4]

The highlight of this period for Weizmann undoubtedly came in April 1925 with the inauguration of Hebrew University on Mount Scopus, the project he had lovingly nurtured for nearly a quarter of a century. The Weizmanns were accompanied to Palestine by Balfour, at the age of 77 and a poor sailor, paying his first visit to the country with which his name had come to be associated. The inauguration ceremony on 1 April was attended by many Jewish dignitaries, including Dr Judah Magnes, who was to be its first Chancellor and later President, but whose work on behalf of Arab-Jewish co-operation in the government of Palestine soon led to bitter recriminations by Weizmann, and alienated him from the mainstream of Zionism.[5] Samuel and Allenby were also present, but inevitably the spotlight fell on Balfour. As expected, the author of the Declaration was rapturously received by a crowd of some 10,000, as he was in Tel Aviv and the Jewish settlements he visited. The Arabs of Palestine, on the other hand, greeted his arrival with a one-day strike, but much worse was to follow when he attempted a somewhat ill-advised visit to Damascus. A crowd of about 6,000 advanced on his hotel and had to be dispersed by the French army, leaving three dead. Balfour's visit to Syria ended almost as soon as it began. Balfour was no better loved by the Arabs than he had been by the Irish, it seemed.[6]

The comparative lull which settled on Palestine for much of the 1920s ended abruptly in 1928. Samuel's tenure as High Commission finished in 1925, being succeeded by Field-Marshal Lord Plumer of Messines, one of Britain's more successful commanders in the War. Between them, Samuel and Plumer managed to keep the political situation relatively calm, but political advance in Egypt, Iraq and Syria led to the Arabs of Palestine feeling left behind. Tension came to a head on 24 September 1928, Yom Kippur, the Jewish Day of Atonement, and it derived from the complex agreements and conventions which had come to surround the Western Wall. For centuries Jews had been allowed access to it, provided that nothing was erected on the pavement, and the British felt obliged to maintain this position. When the Jews put up a screen to separate men from women, the police forcibly took it down. In an atmosphere of increasing tension, each side protested to the League of Nations.[7]

This incident, disturbing as it was, was but the portent of a much more serious sequence of events the following year. The immediate prelude, perhaps, was the culmination of negotiations Weizmann had been pursuing for a number of years, that is, the creation of an enlarged Jewish Agency, which had been provided for in the terms of the Mandate. This was at last agreed at the Sixteenth Zionist Congress in Zurich in the summer of 1929. The Jewish Agency was to be representative of both Zionist and non-Zionist Jews, with Weizmann as its President. In any other circumstances, this would have marked a new high point in his career, but within days any sense of satisfaction he might have felt was shattered by events in Palestine. On 15 August 1929, there was a Jewish procession to the Western Wall; the next day the Arabs followed suit. Then, from 23 to 29 August, there were attacks on Jews across Palestine. In all, 133 Jews were killed and 339 wounded, while 116 Arabs were killed and 232 wounded, most of them by the security forces. Particularly disturbing was the fact that these attacks took place in the ancient Jewish holy cities of Hebron, where some 60 people were killed, and Safed. Jews had lived there for generations, untouched.

The Commission of Enquiry into these events, chaired by Sir Walter Shaw, reported its findings on 31 March 1930, just days after Weizmann had mourned the death of Balfour.[8] The subsequent *Report* pointed to the fundamental differences in outlook between Arabs and Jews, but identified the basic reason behind the outbreak as being Arab fears over the level of Jewish immigration and the amount of land purchase. Shaw's recommendations were that the government should define what it meant by safeguarding the interests of the non-Jewish communities; revise the regulation of immigration, which he described as excessive; institute an enquiry into methods of cultivation and regulate land policy in the light of this; and emphasise once again that the Zionist Organisation could not take part in the government of Palestine.[9]

Weizmann had for some time sensed the hostility of Ramsay MacDonald's Colonial Secretary, Lord Passfield, better known as Sydney Webb, a veteran socialist perhaps best remembered for his work in founding the London School of Economics, and who, with his wife, subsequently wrote a highly sympathetic account of Stalin's Russia. The conclusions of the Commission did not, therefore, come as a complete surprise to Weizmann, unpalatable though they were. Receiving the Report in advance, Weizmann arranged a meeting with MacDonald and Passfield, at which he was joined by Lord Reading, Lord Melchett and Felix Warburg. MacDonald apparently confided his belief that Shaw had exceeded his brief, promising to make a statement to the House of Commons reaffirming British commitment to the National Home, which he did, being supported by Baldwin on behalf of the Conservatives and Lloyd George for the Liberals.[10] Weizmann was also in contact with Baldwin and Lloyd George, and, then, on 11 April the *Manchester Guardian* published Weizmann's lengthy riposte to Shaw, written in his capacity as President of the Jewish Agency. Reasserting that the Jews were in Palestine as of right, he responded that to restrict immigration and land purchase would set at nought the creation of the National Home.[11]

The government announced a further commission, under

Sir John Hope Simpson, to carry forward the enquiry Shaw had recommended. Weizmann had hoped instead for the chairmanship of Smuts, whose sympathies he knew, and at a rather bitter meeting with MacDonald and Passfield he denounced the latter as a liar for reneging on a promise that he could meet Hope Simpson prior to his departure.[12] News that immigration into Palestine had been suspended was a further unwelcome indication of the drift of events, followed, as it was, by amendments to land legislation, and restrictions on the work of the Jewish Agency.[13]

The best that Weizmann could do in the circumstances was try to anticipate through contacts with Passfield what the government's likely reaction might be. By the beginning of October he believed that there would be a five-year ban on land purchases, limits on Jewish immigration, and a loan to settle landless Arabs. His rather pessimistic conclusion was that Passfield, as he had recently done in Kenya with the Africans, would assert the rights of the Arabs as the indigenous population of the country.[14] On 13 October, he wrote to Passfield and MacDonald protesting that any prohibition on land purchases would undermine the National Home, and acknowledge that the Arabs had the greater claim to Palestine. He argued that such a policy would run counter to the Balfour Declaration and the provisions of the Mandate.[15]

Hope Simpson's report, published on 21 October and seen by Weizmann in advance, threatened to undermine one of the main planks of the Zionist platform; namely, that there was sufficient cultivable land to accommodate them without prejudice to the Arabs. Hope Simpson thought not, concluding that until there was further development of Jewish lands and better cultivation of Arabs lands, there was no room for any more settlers if the standard of living of the Arab cultivators were to be maintained. More optimistic from the Zionist perspective was his view that through development the countryside could not only sustain the present population, but accommodate at least an additional 20,000 families of settlers. The Report was accompanied by a Statement of Policy which accepted Hope Simpson's figures and conclusions, but pointedly ignored his view that with development the land could absorb more Jewish immigrants.[16] The Passfield White Paper, as it soon became known, came as a devastating blow to the Zionists, and to Weizmann in particular, for whom co-operation with Britain had been the *sine qua non* of Zionist strategy. His response was that the White Paper dealt a serious blow to prospects for the National Home, and was contrary to the policy set out in the 1922 White Paper. Complaining to Passfield that by issuing a Statement of Policy the government had precluded negotiations, he announced his resignation as President of the Zionist Organisation and the Jewish Agency. To MacDonald, more in sorrow than in anger, he lamented the failure of his policy of working in harmony with the British government.[17]

Weizmann had long castigated the British administration in Palestine for being pro-Arab, but now he had to contend with the Colonial Office as well. As he began his lobbying campaign against the White Paper, he was probably correct in his suspicion that MacDonald was more sympathetic than Passfield. As well as mobilising support in Jewish circles, he enlisted his old friends Amery and Smuts, and the Conservatives Baldwin and Austen Chamberlain also joined in criticising the White Paper. MacDonald sought to defuse the issue by appointing a Cabinet Committee on Palestine, which would examine the question in consultation with the Jewish Agency. Despite his resignation as President, Weizmann co-operated fully throughout the winter of 1930/1, emphasising that the National Home could not be curtailed at its current level, and that the Jews had been the victims in 1929.[18] His reward came on 13 February 1931 in the form of a letter addressed to him from MacDonald, which, while it did not rescind the White Paper, substantially qualified it. In his letter, MacDonald challenged the view that the White Paper 'foreshadows a policy which is inconsistent with the obligations of the Mandatory to the Jewish people'. Emphasising that the Mandate put obligations on Britain towards both Arabs and Jews, he denied that there was any intention to end Jewish land purchases. On the even more vexed question of immigration, he reiterated the long-standing policy of absorptive capacity, confirming that the government did 'not contemplate any stoppage or prohibition of Jewish immigration in any of its categories'.[19]

Once again, Weizmann had succeeded, but this time rather against the odds, and the whole episode had raised questions about his reliance on British good intentions. His critics, especially Jabotinsky's Revisionists, assailed him for accepting a letter rather than another White Paper. This accusation was as unjust as it was wrong-headed, since MacDonald's letter opened up the possibility of immigration into Palestine just as the Jews of Europe were to need it most. The sequel was that at the Zionist Conference in Basel in July 1931, Weizmann's opponents managed to pass a motion of no confidence in him. It was the lowest point in his political career, thus far.[20]

After such a bitter rebuff, it is hardly surprising that Weizmann turned for consolation to the other passion of his life, chemistry. Although he did not cut himself off entirely from Zionism, he built a small laboratory in London, and then another opportunity to revive his scientific career presented itself. This opening was the Daniel Sieff Research Institute at Rehovoth, funded by Weizmann's friend Israel Sieff in memory of his son, and inaugurated in April 1934. Here the Weizmanns built their home in Palestine, a classic piece of modern architecture, designed by Erich (later Eric) Mendelsohn, one of Germany's leading architects, who had recently left the country.[21] After the tribulations he had just come through, this might have seemed an idyllic interlude in Weizmann's life when he could turn to domestic and scientific matters, except for the reason Mendelsohn had left Germany: the coming to power of Adolf Hitler on 30 January 1933.

Hitler, an Austrian who had absorbed the anti-Semitic atmosphere of pre-1914 Vienna and who had harped on the so-called injustices of the Versailles settlement, was barely in power before he began the systematic exclusion of Jews, hitherto amongst the most patriotic of Germans, from national life. What followed hardly needs repetition: the Nuremberg Laws of 1935, the atrocities against the Viennese Jews which followed the Austrian *Anschluss* in 1938, the *Reichskristallnacht* of November 1938, culminating in Hitler's Reichstag speech of 30 January 1939 in which he foretold the fate of the Jews in the event of war, a conflict he was about to start. The result was an exodus of Jews from Germany and elsewhere in Europe. Since the United States was no longer an option for most of them as a result of the ethnic quotas imposed in the 1924 Immigration Act, Palestine was the obvious choice, made possible by Weizmann's recent intervention with Mac-Donald. The figures speak for themselves. Whereas in 1932, Jews accounted for 180,793 out of a population of 1,052,873, by 1936 this had leapt to 370,483 out of 1,336,518.[22] Moreover, many of these immigrants were middle-class urban

Jews who brought with them the cultural values of Central Europe. Tel Aviv was now a major urban centre of 150,000 people. Emblematic of the changing nature of the *Yishuv* was the arrival in 1936 of the legendary Italian conductor Arturo Toscanini to conduct the fledgling Palestine Orchestra, which had recently been founded, and, as the Israel Philharmonic, later to become one of the world's leading orchestras.[23]

This transformation of the National Home provoked the Arabs into action. On 15 April 1936, a Jew was killed near Nablus and the Arab Revolt began, which lasted until 1939, tying down British forces just at the time when the ambitions of Germany, Italy and Japan were becoming increasingly ominous. The Arab Higher Committee was formed, led by Haj Amin al-Husayni, who was now clearly the leader of the Palestinians. The government's response was to send yet another commission of enquiry, chaired by Lord Peel, sadly ill with cancer, charged with making recommendations which might remove the grievances of both parties. Its most dynamic member was Reginald Coupland, Beit Professor of Colonial History at the University of Oxford, who had already analysed nationality problems in Ireland, Canada and South Africa. There then developed a fascinating dynamic between Coupland and Weizmann, who had returned to the presidency of the World Zionist Organisation in 1935. On 23 December 1936, when Weizmann was giving evidence on behalf of the Jewish Agency, Coupland threw out the suggestion of creating what he called two big areas in Palestine. Then, on 8 January 1937 he developed this concept by setting before Weizmann the idea of partition, which would lead in time to independent Arab and Jewish states. What underpinned Coupland's thinking was his conclusion that Arab civilisation was Asian, while that of the Jews was European, and, that, as a result, their national aspirations were incompatible. Weizmann grasped the significance of what Coupland was saying. What was being suggested was a state, not a National Home, albeit in part of Palestine. He was also aware that despite the growth in Jewish numbers, the Arab population was also expanding, and that the prospect of a Jewish majority was some way off. He also knew that partition would meet with resistance in Zionist ranks, especially since it was felt that the creation of Transjordan had already truncated the National Home.

At the end of January 1937, the two men consulted privately at the agricultural settlement of Nahalal, where Weizmann became convinced that partition offered the best way forward. When the Royal Commission reported on 7 July to the Colonial Secretary, none other than Weizmann's old friend Ormsby-Gore, it was in favour of partition. Rather like Caesar's Gaul, Palestine was to be in three parts: a Jewish state along much of the coast and Galilee; an Arab state in the interior; and Jerusalem retained as a British enclave with a corridor to the coast. This proposal was accepted by the Cabinet and in Parliament, though criticised in debate by the veteran pro-Zionist speakers, Lloyd George, Churchill and Samuel, who saw partition as contrary to the Mandate. Their reservations were more than echoed in influential sections of the Zionist movement, as Weizmann had known from the start they would be.

The dispute within Zionism had unmistakable echoes of the 1903 Uganda crisis, except that this time Weizmann was sitting in Herzl's seat, and it came to a head at the Zionist Congress in Zurich in August. Weizmann was supported by the bulk of European and Palestinian representatives, including Ben-Gurion, who had been initially opposed to partition.

The opposition was spearheaded by Ussishkin, but the real threat came from the United States, whence Weizmann's old feud with Brandeis came back to bite him. Brandeis did not attend the Congress, but at a preparatory meeting with Felix Frankfurter, Rabbi Stephen Wise and Robert Szold, partition was rejected. Wise, however, was not in Europe for long before the realities of the Jewish position in Palestine were impressed upon him, and his position changed. He was the prime architect of the compromise strategy that the Congress approved on 10 August 1937; namely, that the Zionists should reject the Peel Commission recommendations, but should negotiate with the British government for a more favourable scheme. While this formula left the door open for partition, it was a lukewarm endorsement, which was ultimately unhelpful to Weizmann, especially since on 11 September an Arab National Conference at Bludan in Syria totally rejected the scheme. It left the British government with the obvious question of whether they should press ahead with a partition plan neither side seemed really to want.

Buoyed up by an assurance from Ormsby-Gore that in a year's time he would be preparing for the establishment of a Jewish state, Weizmann left for Palestine, but the Colonial Office was a junior player compared with the Foreign Office. With war threatening in Europe and the Mediterranean, the last thing the Foreign Secretary, Anthony Eden, and his Prime Minister, Neville Chamberlain, wanted was a hostile Arab world. At a Cabinet meeting on 22 December 1937, it was decided to send a commission under Sir John Woodhead to explore the implementation of a partition scheme, but with a confidential letter to the effect that he was free to pronounce against it. His *Report* duly did on 9 November 1938, the day the *Reichskristallnacht* was unleashed upon the Jews of Germany. All Weizmann's attempts to influence the commission came to nothing, his view that its purpose had been to justify a course of action already determined being quite correct.[24]

If Weizmann felt that his relations with the British government had touched their nadir, much worse was to follow. In May 1938, Ormsby-Gore, whose pro-Zionism had become an inconvenience, was replaced at the Colonial Office by Malcolm MacDonald, son of the late Prime Minister. Even before Woodhead concluded his work, MacDonald had decided upon a conference to discuss the future of Palestine. The conference, held at St James's Palace, opened on 7 February 1939, and ended on 15 March, just as Hitler was taking over the rump of Czechoslovakia which Chamberlain thought he had saved at Munich the previous September. The conference was predictably inconclusive, but during its course, through, it seems, a clerical error, Weizmann became aware of what MacDonald was planning. There would be an independent Palestine, and limited Jewish immigration for the next five years, but after that immigrants would only be allowed with Arab consent. At the closing session, which Weizmann and Ben-Gurion did not attend, MacDonald outlined his proposal that confirmed what Weizmann had already discovered, but in greater detail; namely, that Palestine would become independent in 10 years, and that 75,000 Jews would be permitted to enter over the next five years, but after that only with Arab agreement. This meant, quite simply, that the Jews could only ever be a minority in the country.[25] These, in essence, were the policies which MacDonald went on to unveil in his White Paper of 17 May 1939. They were rejected by the Palestinian Arabs, despite the extent to which the White Paper favoured them, but they proved enough to help Britain's allies, Abdullah of Transjordan and Ibn Saud of Saudi Arabia, keep the Arab world largely quiescent in the war. It was a sad time for Weizmann, compounded by his mother's death.[26]

The Zionist Congress, which convened in Geneva from 16 to 25 August rejected the White Paper, hardly surprisingly, but its proceedings were overshadowed by the pace of events in Europe. When news came on 23 August of the Nazi-Soviet Pact, it was clear that little short of a miracle would stop Hitler, hell-bent as he was on a war over Poland, home to millions of Jews. Over the next three years, his armies conquered most of continental Europe, and advanced deep into the Soviet Union, including what had been in Tsarist times the Pale of Settlement. What then followed will be forever etched on the record of European civilisation, the systematic extermination of some six million Jews. At a time when so many were suffering, the Weizmanns, too, had their share of tragedy. On 11 February 1942, Michael Weizmann, a pilot in the Royal Air Force, went missing when on anti-U boat patrol over the Bay of Biscay.[27]

Sustained by the vain hope that Michael might yet be found, Weizmann travelled to the United States, his third trip

THE HOLOCAUST
On 30 January 1939, in a speech to the Reichstag, Adolf Hitler foretold the destruction of the Jews of Europe in the event of war. Subsequent conquests, especially that of Poland, put large Jewish communities at his mercy. In the spring of 1941, when planning his attack on the Soviet Union, it seems that instructions were given for the extermination of the Jews, which were confirmed on 31 July 1941 by an order from Hermann Göring to Reinhard Heydrich of the SS to proceed to a 'final solution' of the Jewish question. The mass murder of Jews began by the winter of 1941/2, the plans being consolidated by Heydrich at the Wannsee Conference on 20 January 1942. By the end of the war, some six million Jews had perished, either through shooting or in extermination camps, of which Auschwitz-Birkenau was the most notorious.

of the war. Prior to his departure he had published an article in the influential American journal *Foreign Affairs*, in which he had carried forward the case for a Jewish state when the war ended. Although America's entry into the war assured final victory for the Allies, this was not so apparent in the spring of 1942. Nazi extermination policies towards the Jews were well under way, brought together at the Wannsee Conference of 20 January 1942, although hard information about what was happening did not become public until later that year. The British position in the Middle East, including Palestine, was threatened from two directions, from the north by the German advance into the Caucasus, and in Egypt where the success of the *Afrika Korps* was only halted by General Sir Claude Auchinleck at the First Battle of El Alamein in July. In these depressing circumstances, the American Zionists convened an extraordinary conference at New York's Biltmore Hotel between 6 and 11 May, attended by both Weizmann and Ben-Gurion. The 'Biltmore Program', largely the work of Weizmann's American *protégé*, Meyer Weisgal, called for Palestine to be established as a Jewish Commonwealth.[28] While the Biltmore Program was significant in itself, the event also reflected the growing significance of the United States, and of its Jewish community.

When the war ended, Weizmann's long-standing dominance of Zionist affairs began to ebb. British policy under the Labour government, which came into office in the summer of 1945, adhered stubbornly to the terms of the 1939 White Paper, the Foreign Secretary, Ernest Bevin, and his principal adviser on Palestine, Harold Beeley, incurring Jewish opprobrium as a result. With Hitler's atrocities now fully revealed, Jews were determined to secure their state, and were in no mood to indulge the British. In the circumstances,

Weizmann's reliance on Britain seemed to belong to another age. On 1 October 1945, the three Jewish underground groups in Palestine, the *Haganah*, the *Irgun* and *Leh'i*, began the Jewish Revolt against the Mandate. On the political front, Weizmann seemed a spent force. His relations with Ben-Gurion had become increasingly uneasy since 1942, and he now had a new adversary in Rabbi Abba Hillel Silver, a rising star in American Zionism. His support for partition was not dead, however. At a Zionist Executive in Basel in July 1946, it was agreed that partition could be the basis of a solution.[29] Frustrated by the continuing crisis in Palestine, the British announced plans for a conference in London. The simmering crisis within Zionism came to a head at the Twenty-second Zionist Congress, held at Basel from 9–24 December 1946. It was the first since 1939, and in his presidential address Weizmann mourned the six million fellow Jews who had been murdered. Castigating the 1939 White Paper, he expressed understanding for the temper of the young Palestinian Jews, but still condemned violence as something alien to Zionism, and pleaded for restraint. The only way forward, he argued, was the establishment of a Jewish state. But the times were not with him. Now dominated by the representatives of Palestinian and American Zionism, the Congress voted to boycott the London conference, which had already got under way in September without them, or, indeed, the Arabs. Weizmann, who had advocated taking part, took this as a vote of no-confidence and resigned the presidency. He never again attended a Zionist Congress.[30]

Despite spurning him, Zionism had not finished with Weizmann. When the London conference reconvened in January 1947, the Palestinian Arabs attended, and the Jewish Agency, despite the December vote, came for what, with some sophistry, they called informal talks. Partition was now top of the agenda, but the Arabs were adamantly opposed, as always, and the Jewish Agency was too Delphic in its attitude for the British to proceed along this path. Unable to see a way forward, in February, the British government agreed to hand over the future of Palestine to the United Nations. On 15 May, the United Nations Special Committee on Palestine (UNSCOP) was established. Consisting of representatives of Guatemala, Uruguay, Peru, Australia, Canada, Sweden, the Netherlands, Czechoslovakia, Yugoslavia, India and Iran, it was charged with making recommendations for the future of Palestine by 1 September. The Arabs decided to boycott its proceedings, but the Jews made no such mistake. The first task confronting the Zionist leaders was to convince UNSCOP that the British Mandate should end. This was brilliantly accomplished with the refugee ship, *Exodus 1947*, which was intercepted by the Royal Navy on 17 July. Two days later, two members of UNSCOP watched its passengers disembarking at Haifa prior to their return to Germany.

On the more crucial question of the future of Palestine, the Zionist movement was still committed to the 1942 Biltmore Program, which had called for the country to be a Jewish Commonwealth, but privately Ben-Gurion had concluded that partition was the more realistic option. Weizmann, of course, had been its advocate since 1937. When Ben-Gurion presented the Jewish Agency's case before UNSCOP in Jerusalem, he did not mention partition. This was left to Weizmann, who testified on 8 July 1947. Arguing that partition would mean a sacrifice for the Zionists, he conceded that they knew they could not have the whole of Palestine. He appealed for a more generous line than the one offered in the Peel Commission Report by including the Negev Desert in a

Jewish state. It was a clear signal to UNSCOP of what the Zionists would accept. Recalled before the committee, Ben-Gurion confirmed that they would consider a Jewish state in an área less than the whole of Palestine; privately, he assured them that he would support partition, provided he got the Negev.[31]

When UNSCOP reported on 1 September, its members recommended the termination of the Mandate. On the future of Palestine, there was less agreement. The Indian, Iranian and Yugoslav members supported a binational federal state, the Australian could not support any scheme, while the majority ruled in favour of partition. There was to be an Arab state, a Jewish state, a *corpus separatum* for Jerusalem, and economic unity. The Jewish state was to include the Negev, as Weizmann had argued. The Arabs, backed by the British, rejected partition, while the Jews, strongly supported by the Americans, worked assiduously to achieve it. The Americans, however, were concerned that the projected Jewish state contained too many Arabs, and the obvious way to reduce this was to exclude the Negev with its Bedouin population. Faced with this prospect, the Zionists turned again to their old warhorse. On 19 November, Weizmann met President Harry S Truman at the White House. Persuaded by Weizmann that the Negev was vital to the Jewish state, Truman issued immediate instructions to his delegation at the United Nations that it should not be assigned to the Arab state. Not only was this an important intervention, but the impression Weizmann had made on Truman was to prove even more invaluable the following year. When the Ad Hoc Committee on the Palestinian Question took the vote on partition on 25 November 1947, it was supported by 25 votes to 13, with 17 abstentions and two absentees. This vote was some way short of the

two-thirds majority needed to make it a formal recommen-
dation of the General Assembly, where the vote was due to
be taken on the 29th. Once again, Weizmann was brought
into action, successfully telegraphing his friend Leon Blum
to get France's vote changed to one of support for partition. In fact, it took direct action from the White House to
secure a change in intention by enough states, so that when
the vote was held, partition passed by the necessary majority
of 33 votes to 13, with 10 abstentions. Exactly 50 years after
the first Zionist Congress, sanc-
tion had been given for a Jewish
state, and Weizmann was given a
rapturous reception at a rally in
New York.[32]

His services were not yet at
an end, however. With the Arabs
resolutely opposed to partition,
and the British determined not
to implement it, the situation in
Palestine deteriorated dramatically. While partition had been
strongly supported by Truman
and his advisers, this was far
from the case amongst key officials in the Department of
State, and events in the country in early 1948 enabled them
to mount a campaign against it. What they recommended
was that if the United Nations resolution could not be imple-
mented, then the question of Palestine should be referred
back to the General Assembly. Truman agreed to this in principle, though with the *caveat* that he should see the final draft
of any speech. Irritated as he was by the amount of lobbying
he had been subjected to on the issue of Palestine, he gave

HARRY S TRUMAN (1884–1972)
As President of the United States
from the death of Franklin D
Roosevelt on 12 April 1945 until
1953, Truman presided over the
end of the Second World War,
including the decision to drop
atomic bombs on Japan. With the
announcement of the co-called
'Truman Doctrine' in 1947, he was
instrumental in formulating
American policy in what became
known as the Cold War. He took
great pride in his contribution to
the emergence of Israel, which
was considerable.

instructions that no more Zionist leaders were to see him, and that included Weizmann. Knowing nothing of the State Department's campaign against partition, but sensing the coldness coming from the White House, the Zionist leaders searched for a way through the embargo. The key proved to be Eddie Jacobson, Truman's old army comrade and business partner from Kansas City. On 13 March 1948, Jacobson saw Truman at the White House. Comparing him with Truman's political hero, Andrew Jackson, he persuaded an initially reluctant President to meet Weizmann. The subsequent meeting on 19 March, at which no minutes were kept, proved crucial, with Truman reassuring Weizmann that he still supported partition. The following day, unaware of this development, Warren Austin made a speech to the Security Council in which the United States repudiated partition, casting doubt on the prospects for a Jewish state. Jewish opinion, equally ignorant of the White House meeting, was outraged, but as the controversy swirled around the White House, Weizmann kept silent, trusting in Truman's good faith, and earning the President's goodwill in the process. It was not the least of Weizmann's services to Zionism.[33]

When the British Mandate for Palestine ended on 14 May 1948, Ben-Gurion proclaimed the establishment of the State of Israel in the Tel-Aviv museum; 11 minutes later it was accorded *de facto* recognition by Truman. The following day, the new state was attacked by the armies of the Arab League, beginning a war which was to end in February 1949 with Israel's victory. Still in New York, Weizmann was not present at these historic events. On 17 May, he received the news that the Provisional Council of State led by Ben-Gurion had elected him President, and this was subsequently confirmed in Israel's first election in January 1949. To become

EXTRACTS FROM THE DECLARATION OF THE ESTABLISHMENT OF THE STATE OF ISRAEL, 14 MAY 1948.

In the year 5657 (1897), at the summons of the spiritual father of the Jewish State, Theodore Herzl, the first Zionist Congress convened and proclaimed the right of the Jewish people to national rebirth in its own country.

This right was recognised in the Balfour Declaration of the 2nd November 1917, and re-affirmed in the Mandate of the League of Nations which, in particular, gave international sanction to the historic connection between the Jewish people and Eretz-Israel and to the right of the Jewish people to rebuild its National Home.

ACCORDINGLY WE, MEMBERS OF THE PEOPLE'S COUNCIL, REPRESENTATIVES OF THE JEWISH COMMUNITY OF ERETZ-ISRAEL AND OF THE ZIONIST MOVEMENT, ARE HERE ASSEMBLED ON THE DAY OF THE TERMINATION OF THE BRITISH MANDATE OVER ERETZ-ISRAEL AND, BY VIRTUE OF OUR NATURAL AND HISTORIC RIGHT AND ON THE STRENGTH OF THE RESOLUTION OF THE UNITED NATIONS GENERAL ASSEMBLY, HEREBY DECLARE THE ESTABLISHMENT OF A JEWISH STATE IN ERETZ-ISRAEL, TO BE KNOWN AS THE STATE OF ISRAEL.

Source: Israel Ministry of Foreign Affairs

the first President of the State of Israel should have been the triumphant finale to Weizmann's career, but it proved instead to be a coda played out in a minor key. Before returning to Israel, he performed one last service. At an official meeting with Truman on 23 May, Weizmann learned that the United States was willing to make a loan of $100 million to the new state. But he was not long home when the picture darkened. Despite his age and growing infirmity, Weizmann had hoped to play an active part in affairs as President, along the lines of certain continental European countries. Ben-Gurion, for his part, was determined that the role of the President should, like that of the British monarch, be purely symbolic, precisely the word Foreign Minister Moshe Sharett used, with rather insulting honesty, when describing its functions to Weizmann. He was not consulted by Ben-Gurion's government on affairs of state, nor was his request to receive Cabinet minutes granted. Of particular chagrin was the omission of his signature from the Declaration of the Establishment of the State of Israel. He had, of course, not been present in Tel-Aviv at the time, but it galled him that there were 34 signatories to the historic document, and that space had been left for three others who had been absent, although not for him. At best, it seemed a curious omission of the man who had guided Zionism through its pivotal phase, and who was the first President of the State.[34]

He was honoured, of course, but that was not what he had wanted. He made one final visit to the United States in 1949 on behalf of his beloved institute, now named after him, but it was as 'The Prisoner of Rehovoth' that he now saw himself. For the final year of his life, Weizmann was almost entirely confined to his bed. On 9 November 1952, he died.[35]

How, then, may we judge his legacy and career? The State of Israel, which he did so much to bring into existence had, 60 years after its foundation, become a modern, vibrant state with a population of some 7.1 million, 76 per cent of whom are Jews and the rest Arabs. But Israel never found true peace for long. The war of 1948–9 was followed by others in 1956, 1967, 1973, 1982 and 2006. The 1967 war brought the remaining parts of pre-1948 Palestine under Israeli occupation, and while the Palestinian Authority came into being in 1994, a two-state solution remains to be negotiated. For the Palestinians, the events of 1948–9 were *Al-Nakba*, 'The Catastrophe', confounding their hopes of national independence, and making 750,000 of them refugees, their numbers rising in time to some 4.6 million.[36] In 1987 and 2000, *Intifadas*, or uprisings, took place in the occupied territories. A history of the Israeli-Palestinian conflict after Weizmann's death lies far beyond the scope of this volume, but its intractability is a matter of record.

It was Weizmann's great good fortune that the three abiding passions of his life, Zionism, science and England, came together at a unique moment in history, but it was his political genius which allowed him to grasp the possibilities that this opened up. Without his courtship of Balfour and Lloyd George, which had an almost feline quality to it, the Declaration of 1917 is hardly conceivable.[37] It was a skill he never lost, as President Truman was to find three decades later. When Weizmann came to the Paris Peace Conference to put the case for a British Mandate for Palestine, he still faced difficulties, since the French had their own ambitions while Arab opposition to Zionism was already apparent, but in the British he had a ready audience. Even the sceptical Curzon came round in the end, as he showed at San Remo. Brief though his appearance before the Supreme Council might have been, it nonetheless set down the essential marker for the creation of the National Home under the auspices of the British Mandate. In the view of Sir Charles Webster, *doyen* of international historians in the United Kingdom and Secretary to the Military Section of the British Delegation at Paris, what was accomplished at the Conference made British rule in Palestine and the resulting National Home which followed inevitable.[38]

Aware as he was of Arab feelings towards Zionism, Weizmann built too much on his relationship with Feisal, who became a sacrifice to imperial ambition. By then, the Palestinian Arabs were finding their own voice. They felt betrayed by the British and threatened by the Zionists. Although they never really discovered how to deal with either, the Palestinians did force the British into modifying what they meant by the National Home, firstly in the Churchill White Paper in 1922, and more fundamentally in the 1939 White Paper, which the Jews understandably regarded as an act of gross betrayal at the time of their deepest peril. By 1945, the situation had changed beyond recognition, not least because of the Holocaust, and both Zionists and Palestinians had to operate in a world where power had shifted from London to Washington.

Weizmann embraced the British Empire at the height of its power, but as it declined his ability to influence events seemed to wane with it. His rejection by the Zionist movement in 1931 and 1946 was the result of what was felt to be his excessive reliance on Britain's good intentions.[39] Weizmann's relations with many of his fellow Jews, whether assimilationists like Montagu and Levi, or, more importantly, leading Zionists like Brandeis, Jabotinsky, Ussishkin and Silver, were problematic at best, sulphurous at worst, and were in sharp contrast to his ability to persuade non-Jews like Lloyd George and Balfour. Even so, in one of his last speeches, his opening address to the Israeli Constituent Assembly, he concluded by paying generous tribute to the Zionist leaders who had gone before, including Ussishkin and Brandeis, but not, it must have been noted, Jabotinsky, whose ideology was not to his taste.[40] Nor were his relations with Herzl and Ben-Gurion entirely straightforward, but the Zionist movement had been served by three giants, and Chaim Weizmann was by no means the least of them.

Notes

NB. Crown Copyright materials are published with the permission of the Controller of Her Majesty's Stationery Office.

1: From the Pale of Settlement to the Pursuit of Zion

1. Chaim Weizmann, *Trial and Error. The Autobiography of Chaim Weizmann* (Hamish Hamilton, London: 1949) pp 11–27; Jehuda Reinharz, *Chaim Weizmann. The Making of a Zionist Leader* (Oxford University Press, New York and Oxford: 1985) p 7; Norman Rose, *Chaim Weizmann. A Biography* (Weidenfeld and Nicolson, London: 1986) pp 16–18.
2. Weizmann, *Trial and Error*, pp 13–14.
3. Weizmann to Shlomo Tsvi Sokolovsky, Motol, Summer 1885, in Leonard Stein (ed), *The Letters and Papers of Chaim Weizmann*, Series A Letters, Volume I Summer 1885–29 October 1902 (Oxford University Press, London: 1968) 1, pp 35–7, hereafter *LPCW*.
4. Weizmann, *Trial and Error*, pp 34–5.
5. Weizmann, *Trial and Error*, pp 38–40.
6. Reinharz, *Chaim Weizmann. The Making of a Zionist Leader*, pp 35–6.

7. Weizmann, *Trial and Error*, pp 44–50.
8. Weizmann, *Trial and Error*, pp 69 and 76; Reinharz, *Chaim Weizmann. The Making of a Zionist Leader*, p 51; Rose, *Chaim Weizmann*, p 44.
9. Walter Laqueur, *A History of Zionism* (Schocken Books, New York: 1989 edition) pp 80–1.
10. Alex Bein, *Theodore Herzl* (The Jewish Publication Society of America, Philadelphia: 1941) pp 112–16.
11. See Theodore Herzl, *The Jewish State. An Attempt at a Modern Solution of the Jewish Question* (H. Pordes, London: 1972, sixth edition, revised with foreword by Israel Cohen; original edition, 1896).
12. 'The Basle Declaration', in Walter Laqueur (ed), *The Israel-Arab Reader* (Pelican Books, London: 1970) pp 28–9; *Laqueur, A History of Zionism*, pp 103–8.
13. Weizmann, *Trial and Error*, pp 51–2.
14. Leonard Stein, *The Balfour Declaration* (The Magnes Press, The Hebrew University, The Jewish Chronicle Publications: Jerusalem, London: 1983; original edition 1961) pp 90–1.
15. Weizmann, *Trial and Error*, pp 61–8.
16. Weizmann, *Trial and Error*, pp 80–1.
17. Professor Hugo Bergmann, 'Dr. Weizmann's conception of the Hebrew University', in Paul Goodman (ed), *Chaim Weizmann. A Tribute on his Seventieth Birthday*, (Victor Gollancz Ltd, London: 1945) p 94; Reinharz, *Chaim Weizmann. The Making of a Zionist Leader*, pp 86–91.
18. Weizmann to Theodor Herzl, Vienna, 21 May 1902; Weizmann to Theodor Herzl, Vienna, 4 June 1902; Weizmann to Theodor Herzl, Vienna, 25 June 1902; *LPCW*, Volume I, 204, 207, 209, pp 263–9.

19. Weizmann, *Trial and Error*, pp 103–5.
20. Weizmann, *Trial and Error*, p 145; Vera Weizmann, *The Impossible Takes Longer. Memoirs by the Wife of Israel's First President as Told to David Tutaev* (Hamish Hamilton, London: 1967) pp 1–3, 12–13.
21. Bein, *Theodore Herzl*, pp 439–41.
22. Weizmann, *Trial and Error*, pp 110–17.
23. Bein, *Theodore Herzl*, pp 453–503.
24. Weizmann, *Trial and Error*, p 146.
25. Weizmann, *Trial and Error*, pp 123–34.
26. Vera Weizmann, *The Impossible Takes Longer*, pp 30–5.
27. Vera Weizmann, *The Impossible Takes Longer*, pp 30–5; Rose, *Chaim Weizmann*, p 113.
28. Blanche E C Dugdale, *Arthur James Balfour. First Earl of Balfour* (Hutchinson, London: 1936) Volume I, pp 325–6; Weizmann, *Trial and Error*, p 142.
29. Weizmann, *Trial and Error*, pp 142–5; Dugdale, *Arthur James Balfour*, Volume I, pp 326–7; Reinharz, *Chaim Weizmann. The Making of a Zionist Leader*, pp 270–5.
30. Reinharz, *Chaim Weizmann. The Making of a Zionist Leader*, pp 275–7.
31. Stein, *The Balfour Declaration*, pp 80–1.
32. Weizmann, *Trial and Error*, pp 173–4; Vera Weizmann, *The Impossible Takes Longer*, p 39; Reinharz, *Chaim Weizmann. The Making of a Zionist Leader*, pp 359–67; David Vital, *Zionism: The Crucial Phase* (Clarendon Press, Oxford: 1987) pp 120–1.

2: Palestine under the Ottomans

1. Weizmann, *Trial and Error*, pp 161–9; Reinharz, *Chaim Weizmann. The Making of a Zionist Leader*, pp 316–17.
2. Weizmann, *Trial and Error*, p 161.

3. Frank Adams, 'Palestine Agriculture', in *Palestine: A Decade of Development, The Annals of the American Academy of Political and Social Science* (November 1932) pp 72–83.

4. Adams, 'Palestine Agriculture', pp 72–83.

5. Philip Mattar, *The Mufti of Jerusalem. Al-Hajj Amin Al-Husayni and the Palestinian National Movement* (Columbia University Press, New York: 1988) pp 6–7.

6. Albert Hourani, *A History of the Arab Peoples* (The Belknap Press of Harvard University Press, Cambridge, Massachusetts: 1991) pp 308–10; Ilan Pappe, *A History of Modern Palestine. One Land, Two Peoples* (Cambridge University Press, Cambridge: 2004) pp 45–6.

7. Laqueur, *A History of Zionism*, pp 75–9.

8. David Ben-Gurion, *Recollections*, edited by Thomas R Bransten (Macdonald Unit 75, London: 1970) pp 60–1.

9. Dr Yehuda Slutsky, 'Under Ottoman Rule (1880–1917)', in Israel Pocket Library, *History from 1880* (Keter Publishing House, Jerusalem: 1973) p 17.

10. Professor Hugo Bergman, 'Dr. Weizmann's Conception of the Hebrew University'; Weizmann, 'A Jewish University', Eleventh Zionist Congress, Vienna, September 1913, in Goodman, *Chaim Weizmann*, pp 93–107, 149–52.

11. Weizmann, *Trial and Error*, pp 176–85.

3: War and the Balfour Declaration

1. Sir Charles Kingsley Webster, *The Founder of the National Home* (Yad Chaim Weizmann, Rehovoth: 1955) pp 16–17.

2. The Rt. Hon. Viscount Samuel, *Memoirs* (The Cresset Press, London: 1945) p 139.

3. Samuel, *Memoirs*, pp 140–1; Vital, *Zionism: The Crucial Phase* pp 92–3.

4. Weizmann, *Trial and Error*, pp 190–1; Weizmann to Ahad Ha'am, London, 12 November 1914; Weizmann to Charles P Scott, Manchester, 12 November 1914, Leonard Stein (ed), *LPCW*, Series A, Volume VII (Oxford University Press, London and New York: 1975), 32, 33, pp 37–9.

5. Trevor Wilson (ed), *The Political Diaries of C. P. Scott 1911–1928* (Collins, London: 1970) p 113.

6. Weizmann to Vera Weizmann, Manchester, 10 December 1914; Weizmann to Charles P Scott, Manchester, 13 December 1914, *LPCW*, Volume VII, 65, 67, pp 77–80.

7. Weizmann, *Trial and Error*, pp 192–3; Reinharz, *Chaim Weizmann. The Making of a Statesman*, pp 24–5.

8. Weizmann to Yehiel Tschlenow and Nahum Sokolow, London, 20 March 1915, *LPCW*, Volume VII, 141, pp 178–9; Stein, *The Balfour Declaration*, pp 107–111.

9. Weizmann to Charles P Scott, Manchester, 23 March 1915; Weizmann to Yehiel Tschlenow and Nahum Sokolow, London, 15 April 1915, *LPCW*, Volume VII, 147, 154, pp 183–5, 190–1.

10. Slutsky, 'Under Ottoman Rule (1880–1917)', pp 24–7.

11. L S Amery, *My Political Life*, Volume Two, *War and Peace, 1914–1929* (Hutchinson, London: 1953) pp 117–18; John Henry Patterson, *The Man-Eaters of Tsavo* (Digireads.com Publishing, Stilwell: 2005, original edition 1907); Patterson's East African adventures are vividly portrayed in the 1996 film, *The Ghost and the Darkness*.

12. Avi Shlaim, *The Iron Wall. Israel and the Arab World* (Penguin Books, London: 2000) p 11; Rose, *Chaim Weizmann*, pp 131–3.

13. T G Fraser, 'The Middle East: partition and reformation', in Seamus Dunn and T G Fraser (eds), *Europe and Ethnicity. The First World War and contemporary ethnic conflict* (Routledge, London and New York: 1996) p 163.

14. *Correspondence between Sir Henry McMahon and the Sharif Hussein of Mecca*, July 1915-March 1916 (Cmd. 5957, London: 1939), Crown Copyright, in T G Fraser, *The Middle East 1914–1979* (Edward Arnold, London: 1980) pp 12–13.

15. Sir Henry McMahon to Sir John Shuckburgh, 12 March 1922, in Martin Gilbert, *Winston S. Churchill*, Volume IV, Companion, Part 3, Documents, April 1921–November 1922 (Heinemann, London: 1977) p 1805; Samuel, *Memoirs*, pp 172–3.

16. George Antonius, *The Arab Awakening* (Librairie du Liban, Beirut: 1969, original edition Hamish Hamilton, London: 1938) pp 168–79.

17. Fraser, 'The Middle East: partition and reformation', p 166.

18. David Lloyd George, *War Memoirs*, two volume edition (Odhams Press Limited, London: 1938) Volume I, pp 112–17.

19. Weizmann, *Trial and Error*, pp 218–22; Wilson (ed), *The Political Diaries of C. P. Scott*, p 128; Lloyd George, *War Memoirs*, Volume I, pp 347–8; Reinharz, *Chaim Weizmann. The Making of a Statesman*, pp 40–72; Rose, *Chaim Weizmann*, pp 152–8.

20. Lloyd George, *War Memoirs*, Volume I, p 349; The Rt. Hon. The Earl Lloyd George of Dwyfor, O.M., 'Foreword', in Paul Goodman (ed), *Chaim Weizmann. A Tribute on his Seventieth Birthday* (Victor Gollancz Ltd, London: 1945); Reinharz, *Chaim Weizmann. The Making of a Statesman*, pp 67–9.

21. Andrea Bosco and Alex May (eds), *The Round Table, the Empire/Commonwealth and British Foreign Policy* (Lothian Foundation Press, London: 1997) pp i–xv.

22. Weizmann, *Trial and Error*, p 229.

23. UNSCOP Report, Volume III, verbatim hearing of the Twenty-First Meeting (Public), Jerusalem, 8 July 1947, hearing of Dr Weizmann, in Fraser (ed), *The Middle East 1914–1979*, pp 18–20.

24. Stein, *The Balfour Declaration*, pp 362–9.

25. Weizmann, *Trial and Error*, pp 235–6; Stein, *The Balfour Declaration*, pp 368–9.

26. Weizmann to Vladimir Jabotinsky, Hazeley Down, 8 February 1917; Weizmann to C P Scott, Manchester, 20 March 1917, *LPCW*, Volume VII, 306, 321, pp 328–9, 343–5; Weizmann, *Trial and Error*, pp 238–40; Stein, *The Balfour Declaration*, pp 370–4.

27. Weizmann to C P Scott, Manchester, 23 March 1917, *LPCW*, Volume VII, 323, pp 346–7; Weizmann, *Trial and Error*, pp 240–1; Stein, *The Balfour Declaration*, pp 378–85.

28. Isaiah Friedman, *The Question of Palestine 1914–1918. British-Jewish-Arab Relations* (Routledge & Kegan Paul, London: 1973) pp 161–2.

29. Note of Interview with Robert Cecil at the Foreign Office, 25 April 1917, *LPCW*, Volume VII, 356, pp

375–8; Weizmann, *Trial and Error*, pp 241–2; Stein, *The Balfour Declaration*, pp 392–3.

30. Weizmann to Louis D Brandeis, Washington, 23 April 1917, *LPCW*, Volume VII, 351, pp 3771–3; Dugdale, *Arthur James Balfour*, Volume II, pp 169–70.

31. Weizmann, *Trial and Error*, pp 246–51; Reinharz, *Chaim Weizmann. The Making of a Statesman*, pp 153–71.

32. Weizmann to the Editor of *The Times*, London, 27 May 1917, *LPCW*, Volume VII, 405, pp 418–19.

33. Weizmann, *Trial and Error*, pp 352–5; Stein, *The Balfour Declaration*, pp 442–61.

34. Weizmann to Sir Ronald Graham, London, 13 June 1917, *LPCW*, Volume VII, 432, pp 438–42.

35. Weizmann to Harry Sacher, Manchester, 20 June 1917, *LPCW*, Volume VII, 435, pp 444–5.

36. *Palestine. A Study of Jewish, Arab, and British Policies* (Published for the Esco Foundation for Palestine, Inc., Yale University Press, New Haven: 1947), Volume I, pp 102–3; Herbert Sidebotham, *Great Britain and Palestine* (Macmillan, London: 1937) p 65.

37. Stein, *The Balfour Declaration*, p 470.

38. Friedman, *The Question of Palestine 1914–1918*, p 257.

39. War Cabinet 227, 3 September 1917, CAB 23/4, in Fraser, *The Middle East 1914–1979*, pp 13–14.

40. Weizmann to Louis D Brandeis, Washington, (?) 12 September 1917, *LPCW*, Volume VII, 496, pp 505–6; Weizmann, *Trial and Error*, pp 257–8; Stein, *The Balfour Declaration*, pp 504–7; Friedman, *The Question of Palestine 1914–1918*, pp 261–3.

41. Weizmann to Philip Kerr, London, 19 September 1917; Weizmann to Nahum Sokolow, Brighton, 30 September 1917, *LPCW*, Volume VII, 507, 513, pp 516, 520.

42. Weizmann to Arthur J Balfour, London, 3 October 1917, *LPCW*, Volume VII, 514, pp 521–2; Weizmann, *Trial and Error*, pp 257–8.

43. War Cabinet 245, 4 October 1917, CAB 23/4, in Fraser, *The Middle East 1914–1979*, pp 15–17; Amery, *My Political Life*, Volume Two, pp 116–17.

44. Weizmann to Louis D Brandeis, Washington, 9 October 1917, *LPCW*, Volume VII, 516, pp 530–1.

45. Brandeis to Jacob de Haas, 17 October 1917, Melvin L Urofsky and David W Levy (eds), *Letters of Louis D. Brandeis*, Volume IV (1916–1921) (State University of New York Press, Albany: 1975) pp 318–19; Stein, *The Balfour Declaration*, pp 528–31.

46. Stein, *The Balfour Declaration*, p 274.

47. War Cabinet 261, 31 October 1917, CAB 23/4, in Fraser, *The Middle East 1914–1979*, pp 17–18; Cmd. 5479, p 22.

48. Weizmann to Lord Rothschild, Tring, 2 November 1917, *LPCW*, Volume VII, 534, pp 541–2.

49. Weizmann to Jacobus H Kann, The Hague, 6 December 1917, Dvorah Barzilay and Barnet Litvinoff (eds), *LPCW*, Series A, Volume VIII (Transaction Books, Rutgers University, Israel Universities Press, Jerusalem: 1977) 21, pp 19–20; Weizmann, *Trial and Error*, p 262; Vera Weizmann, *The Impossible Takes Longer*, p 78; Webster, *The Founder of the National Home*, pp 30–1.

50. Stein, *The Balfour Declaration*, pp 590–1.

4: The Paris Peace Conference

1. Weizmann to Jacob de Haas, New York, (12) December 1917; Weizmann to Sir Mark Sykes, London, 16 January 1918, *LPCW*, Volume VIII, 23, 69, pp 20–1, 62–3; Weizmann, *Trial and Error*, pp 266–7.

2. Weizmann to Vera Weizmann, London, 24–26 March 1918, *LPCW*, Volume VIII, 138, pp 106–9.

3. Weizmann to Vera Weizmann, London, 6 April 1918, *LPCW*, Volume VIII, 151, pp 118–20.

4. Weizmann to William G A Ormsby-Gore, Tel Aviv, 16 April 1918, *LPCW*, Volume VIII, 161, pp 128–30; Ronald Storrs, *Orientations* (Ivor Nicholson & Watson Ltd, London: 1939) p 366.

5. Weizmann to Vera Weizmann, London, 18 April 1918; Weizmann to Louis D Brandeis, Washington, 25 April 1918, *LPCW*, Volume VIII, 163, 175, pp 131–3, 158–67.

6. Weizmann to Vera Weizmann, London, 17 June 1918; Weizmann to Louis D Brandeis, Washington, 23 June 1918, *LPCW*, Volume VII, 213, 215, pp 209–11, 212–3; Weizmann, *Trial and Error*, pp 290–5.

7. Weizmann to Arthur J Balfour, London, 17 July 1918, *LPCW*, Volume VIII, 232, pp 228–32; Reinharz, *Chaim Weizmann. The Making of a Statesman*, pp 295–7.

8. Weizmann to Vera Weizmann, 27 July 1918, *LPCW*, Volume VIII, 236, pp 237–40; Weizmann, *Trial and Error*, pp 295–7.

9. Weizmann to Aaron Aaronsohn, Washington, (22–23) October 1918; Weizmann to Gilbert F Clayton, G.H.Q., Palestine, 27 November 1918, Jehuda Reinharz (ed), *LPCW*, Series A, Volume IX, October 1918–July 1920, (Transaction Books, Rutgers University, Israel Universities Press, Jerusalem: 1977) 1, 38, pp 1, 40–3.

10. Weizmann to Gilbert F Clayton, Palestine, 5 November 1918; Weizmann to David Eder, Tel Aviv-Jaffa, 5 November 1918, *LPCW*, Volume IX, 7, 8, pp 9–20.

11. Weizmann to Louis D Brandeis, Washington, 29 October 1918; Weizmann to David Eder, Tel Aviv-Jaffa, 26 November 1918, *LPCW*, Volume IX, 4, 37, pp 2–8, 39–40.

12. Weizmann to Louis D. Brandeis Washington, 11 November 1918; Weizmann to C P Scott, Manchester, 16 November 1918, *LPCW*, Volume IX, 11, 18, pp 22, 26–7.

13. Weizmann to Lord Robert Cecil, London, 1 November 1918; Appendix 1, 'Proposals submitted by the Zionist Organisation to the Secretary of State for Foreign Affairs regarding matters affecting the Jewish population of Palestine during the Military occupation of that Country', 1 November 1918, *LPCW*, Volume IX, 5, pp 8, 389–90.

14. Weizmann to David Eder, Tel Aviv-Jaffa, 4 December 1918,; Weizmann to Nahum Sokolow, Paris, 5 December 1918, *LPCW*, Volume IX, 52, 53, pp 53–6.

15. Weizmann to Sir Eyre Crowe, London, 16 December 1918, *LPCW*, Volume IX, 70, pp 69–71.

16. 'Feisal-Weizmann Agreement', 3 January 1919, *LPCW*, Volume IX, between pp 86 and 87; Antonius, *The Arab Awakening*, pp 437–9.

17. Rose, *Chaim Weizmann. A Biography*, p 200.

18. Weizmann to Vera Weizmann, London, 8 January 1919, *LPCW*, Volume IX, 100, pp 92–4; Reinharz, *Chaim Weizmann. The Making of a Statesman*, p 296.

19. Weizmann to Sir Arthur Wigram Money, London, 26 January 1919, *LPCW*, Volume IX, pp 104–7.

20. 'Statement of the Zionist Organisation regarding Palestine', 3 February 1919, *LPCW*, Volume IX, Appendix 11, pp 391–402.

21. Weizmann to Vera Weizmann, London, 28 February 1919, *LPCW*, Volume IX, 123, pp 116–19.

22. Weizmann, *Trial and Error*, p 304.

23. M Dockrill (ed), *Supreme Council Minutes, January-March 1919, British Documents on Foreign Affairs: Reports and Papers from the Foreign Office Confidential Print*, General Editors Kenneth Bourne and D Cameron Watt, *Part II, From the First to the Second World War, Series I, The Paris Peace Conference of 1919*, Volume 2, pp 260–1; Weizmann, *Trial and Error*, p 304.

24. Dockrill (ed), *Supreme Council Minutes*, pp 261–2.

25. Dockrill (ed), *Supreme Council Minutes*, pp 262–4.

26. Weizmann, *Trial and Error*, p 205.

27. Dockrill (ed), *Supreme Council Minutes*, pp 264–5.

28. Weizmann, *Trial and Error*, p 306.

29. Weizmann to Vera Weizmann, London, 28 February 1919, *LPCW*, Volume IX, 123, pp 116–19.

30. Esco, *Palestine*, Volume I, pp 161–2.

31. 'At the Peace Conference. Report on March 5th 1919 to the International Zionist Conference held in London', Goodman (ed), *Chaim Weizmann*, pp 158–9.

32. 'At the Peace Conference', Goodman (ed), *Chaim Weizmann*, pp 155–60.

33. Weizmann to Arthur J Balfour, London, *LPCW*, Volume IX, 135, pp 128–32, also footnotes 1, 2 and 3.

34. Weizmann to Israel Sieff, Manchester, 12 April 1919, *LPCW*, Volume IX, 136, pp 132–4.

35. General Clayton, Cairo, to Earl Curzon, 5 June 1919, Enclosures, 'Report by British Liaison Officer on

Political Situation in Arabia', Damascus, 16 May 1919', 'Emir Feisal's Address to the Notables of Syria in the Town Hall of Damascus, the 9 May, 1919, at 3 p.m.', E L Woodward and Rohan Butler (eds), *Documents on British Foreign Policy 1919–1939*, First Series, Volume IV, 1919, Crown Copyright, (Her Majesty's Stationery Office, London: 1952) No. 182, pp 263–72, hereafter *DBFP*.

36. General Clayton, Cairo, to Earl Curzon, 8 June 1919; General Clayton, Cairo, to Earl Curzon, 19 June 1919, *DBFP*, Volume IV, Nos. 183 and 196, pp 272–3, 281–2.

37. Colonel French, Cairo, to Earl Curzon, 26 August 1919, Enclosure,' Arab Movement and Zionism', Major J N Camp, 12 August 1919, *DBFP*, Volume IV, No. 253, pp 360–5.

38. Esco, *Palestine*, Volume I, pp 213–22; Antonius, *The Arab Awakening*, pp 443–58.

39. Earl Curzon to Mr Balfour, Paris, 19 June 1919, Enclosures, 'Letter from Sir W. Tyrrell to Mr Samuel', 31 May 1919; 'Letter from Dr Weizmann to Sir W. Tyrrell', 6 June 1919'; 'Letter from Mr Samuel to Sir W. Tyrrell', 5 June 1919, *DBFP*, Volume IV, No. 197, pp 282–5.

40. Mr Balfour, Paris, to Earl Curzon, 2 July 1919, Enclosure 'Memorandum' for Lloyd George, *DBFP*, Volume IV, No. 211, pp 301–3.

41. 'Note by Sir R. Graham of conversations with Mr. Samuel and Dr. Weizmann', 2 July 1919, *DBFP*, Volume IV, No 213, pp 307–8.

42. Philip Noel Baker to Forbes Adam, 24 July 1919, *DBFP*, Volume IV, No. 227, pp 317–18.

43. Earl Curzon to Colonel French, Cairo, 4 August 1919, *DBFP*, Volume IV, No. 236, p 329.

44. 'Memorandum by Mr. Balfour (Paris) respecting Syria, Palestine, and Mesopotamia', 11 August 1919, *DBFP*, Volume IV, No. 242, pp 340–9.

45. Vera Weizmann, *The Impossible Takes Longer*, pp 91–2.

5: San Remo, the National Home and Arab resistance

1. Weizmann to Robert Vansittart, London, 1 March 1920, *LPCW*, Volume IX, 294, pp 320–2.

2. *Palestine Royal Commission Report* (Cmd. 5479, London: 1937), Crown Copyright.

3. Weizmann to the Zionist Executive, London, 25 March 1920, *LPCW*, Volume IX, pp 325–30.

4. *Palestine Royal Commission Report*, pp 50–1; Mattar, *The Mufti of Jerusalem*, pp 15–8.

5. Weizmann to (Lady) Emma Caroline Schuster, Twyford, Montreux, 3 May 1920, *LPCW*, Volume IX, 318, pp 343–4.

6. Weizmann, *Trial and Error*, pp 318–21.

7. To Vera Weizmann, Launay, 19 April 1920, *LPCW*, Volume IX, 306, pp 336–7.

8. 'British Secretary's Notes of a Meeting of the Supreme Council, held at the Villa Devachan, San Remo, on Saturday, April 24, 1920, at 4 p.m.', Rohan Butler and J P T Bury (eds), *Documents on British Foreign Policy 1919–1939*, First Series, Volume VIII, International Conferences on High Policy, 1920 (Her Majesty's Stationery Office, 1958), Crown Copyright, No. 15, pp 156–71, hereafter *DBFP*.

9. 'British Secretary's Notes of a Meeting of the Supreme Council, held at the Villa Devachan, San Remo, on Sunday, April 25, 1920, at 11 a.m.', *DBFP*, Volume VIII, No. 16, pp 172–7.

10. Weizmann to Vera Weizmann, London, 26 April 1920; Weizmann to the Zionist Bureau, London, 27 April 1920, *LPCW*, Volume IX, 313, 315, pp 340–2; Weizmann, *Trial and Error*, pp 324–5.

11. 'At the First International Zionist Conference after the San Remo Decision, held in London, July 7th, 1920', Goodman, *Chaim Weizmann. A Tribute on his Seventieth Birthday*, pp 160–5.

12. Shabtai Teveth, *Ben-Gurion. The Burning Ground 1886–1948* (Robert Hale Limited, London: 1987) pp 161–4.

13. Weizmann, *Trial and Error*, pp 326–9; Laqueur, *A History of Zionism*, pp 458–9; Reinharz, *Chaim Weizmann. The Making of a Statesman*, pp 327–33.

14. Samuel, *Memoirs*, p 154; Storrs, *Orientations*, p 349; Norman & Helen Bentwich, *Mandate Memories 1918–1948* (The Hogarth Press, London: 1965) p 59.

15. Sir Arnold T Wilson, MP, *Loyalties. Mesopotamia*, Volume II, 1917–1920. *A Personal and Historical Record* (Oxford University Press, London: 1931) pp 310–14.

16. Keith Jeffery, *The British Army and the Crisis of Empire 1918–22* (Manchester University Press, Manchester: 1984) pp 150–1; John Marlowe, *Late Victorian, The Life of Sir Arnold Wilson* (The Cresset Press, London: 1967) pp 212–31.

17. A L Tibawi, *A Modern History of Syria including Lebanon and Palestine,* (Macmillan, London: 1969) pp 318–37.

18. David Fromkin, *A Peace to End All Peace. Creating the modern Middle East 1914–1922* (Penguin Books, London: 1989) pp 501–6.

19. 'Winston S. Churchill: remarks to a Palestinian Arab delegation', 30 March 1921; 'Winston S. Churchill:

remarks to a Zionist delegation', 30 March 1921, Gilbert, *Winston S. Churchill*, Companion, Volume IV, Part 2, Documents July 1919–March 1921, pp 1419–22.

20. Weizmann, *Trial and Error*, pp 326–36; Brandeis to Felix Frankfurter, 26 April 1921, Brandeis to Julian William Mack, 3 June 1921; Brandeis to the Executive Council of the World Zionist Organisation, 19 June 1921, Urofsky and Levy (eds), *Letters of Louis D. Brandeis*, Volume 4, pp 553–4, 562–3, 567–8; Reinharz, *Chaim Weizmann. The Making of a Statesman*, pp 344–50.

21. Mattar, *The Mufti of Jerusalem*, pp 21–7.

22. *Palestine Royal Commission Report*, pp 51–2.

23. Sir Herbert Samuel to Winston S. Churchill, 8 May 1921, Gilbert, *Winston S. Churchill*, Companion, Volume IV, Part 3, Documents April 1921–November 1922, pp 1459–93.

24. Weizmann, *Trial and Error*, pp 342–3.

25. Esco, *Palestine*, Volume I, pp 274–5.

26. Notes of a conversation held at A J Balfour's house, 22 July 1921, Central Zionist Archives, Gilbert, *Winston S. Churchill*, Companion, Volume IV, Part 3, Documents April 1921–November 1922, pp 1558–61.

27. 'Palestine', Winston S. Churchill: Cabinet Memorandum, 11 August 1921; 'Palestine', Colonial Office Memorandum, 11 August 1921, Gilbert, *Winston S. Churchill*, Companion, Volume IV, Part 3, Documents April 1921–November 1922, pp 1585–90.

28. Esco, *Palestine*, Volume I, pp 277–9.

29. Cabinet minutes, CAB 23/26, 18 August 1921, Gilbert, *Winston S. Churchill*, Companion, Volume IV, Part 3, Documents April 1921–November 1922, p 1606.

30. Sir Herbert Samuel to Winston S. Churchill, 14 October 1921, Gilbert, *Winston S. Churchill*, Companion, Volume IV, Part 3, Documents April 1921–November 1922, pp 1650–5.

31. Esco, *Palestine*, Volume I, pp 279–80.

32. Weizmann, *Trial and Error*, pp 350–60.

33. *Statement of British Policy in Palestine, 3 June 1922* (Cmd. 1700, London: 1922), Crown Copyright.

34. Weizmann, *Trial and Error*, pp 360–2; Esco, *Palestine*, Volume I, pp 285–6.

35. Weizmann, *Trial and Error*, pp 363–4.

36. *Palestine Royal Commission Report*, pp 34–40.

6: Weizmann: the prisoner of Zion?

1. Rose, *Chaim Weizmann*, pp 234–7, 245–74.

2. *Palestine Royal Commission Report*, pp 43, 46, 62.

3. Howard M Sachar, *A History of Israel. From the Rise of Zionism to Our Time* (Basil Blackwell, Oxford: 1976) p 155.

4. Teveth, *Ben-Gurion*, pp 187–8.

5. Weizmann to Felix M Warburg, New York, 24 November 1929, Camillo Dresner (ed), *LPCW*, Volume XIV, Series A, July 1929-October 1930 (Transaction Books, Rutgers University, Israel Universities Press, Jerusalem: 1978) 104, p 103.

6. Weizmann, *Trial and Error*, pp 390–400; Dugdale, *Arthur James Balfour*, Volume II, pp 267–72.

7. *Palestine Royal Commission Report*, pp 65–7.

8. Weizmann to Gerald Balfour, Woking, 19 March 1930, *LPCW*, Volume XIV, 225, p 252.

9. *Palestine Royal Commission Report*, pp 67–71.

10. Weizmann to Charles Prestwich Scott, Manchester, 31 March 1930, *LPCW*, Volume XIV, 233, pp 256–7.

11. Weizmann to the Editor of the *Manchester Guardian*, 11 April 1930, *LPCW*, Volume XIV, 248, pp 266–8.

12. Weizmann to Vera Weizmann, Paris, 13 May 1930, *LPCW*, Volume XIV, 269, pp 281–3.

13. Weizmann to James Ramsay MacDonald, London, 16 May 1930, *LPCW*, Volume XIV, 275, pp 300–1.

14. Weizmann to Felix M Warburg, New York, 6 October 1930, *LPCW*, Volume XIV, 357, pp 376–81.

15. Weizmann to Lord Passfield, London, 13 October 1930, *LPCW*, Volume XIV, 359, pp 382–4.

16. *Palestine Royal Commission Report*, pp 71–3.

17. Weizmann to Lord Passfield, London, 21 October 1930; Weizmann to James Ramsay MacDonald, London, 21 October 1930, *LPCW*, Volume XIV, 364, 368, pp 387–9, 391.

18. Weizmann, *Trial and Error*, pp 413–15.

19. J Ramsay MacDonald, House of Commons, 13 February 1931.

20. Weizmann, *Trial and Error*, pp 417–20; Rose, *Chaim Weizmann*, pp 289–93.

21. Rose, *Chaim Weizmann*, pp 294–300.

22. *Report on the Administration of Palestine for 1938*, p 226.

23. Sachar, *A History of Israel*, p 586.

24. For a fuller discussion see: T G Fraser, *Partition in Ireland, India and Palestine: theory and practice* (Macmillan, London and Basingstoke: 1984) Chapter 6, 'Palestine: the Peel Commission'; and T G Fraser, 'A Crisis of Leadership: Weizmann and the Zionist Reactions to the Peel Commission's Proposals, 1937–8',

Journal of Contemporary History, Volume 23, Number 4 (October 1988) pp 657–80.

25. Weizmann, *Trial and Error*, pp 493–501; Rose, *Chaim Weizmann*, pp 344–6.

26. Rose, *Chaim Weizmann*, p 353.

27. Vera Weizmann, *The Impossible Takes Longer*, pp 188–9.

28. Esco, *Palestine*, Volume II, p 1080; Laqueur, *A History of Zionism*, pp 545–7.

29. Fraser, *Partition in Ireland, India and Palestine*, p 156.

30. 'Presidential Address by Dr. Chaim Weizmann', Twenty-Second Zionist Congress, Basle, 9th December 1946' (The Jewish Agency for Palestine, London: nd); Weizmann, *Trial and Error*, pp 543–4; Vera Weizmann, *The Impossible Takes Longer*, pp 211–13; Getzel Kressel, 'Zionist Congresses', Israel Pocket Library, *Zionism* (Keter Publishing House, Jerusalem: 1973) p 253.

31. Fraser, *Partition in Ireland, India and Palestine*, pp 162–3.

32. Fraser, *Partition in Ireland, India and Palestine*, pp 179–82; T G Fraser, *The USA and the Middle East since World War 2* (Macmillan, Basingstoke and London: 1989) pp 31–4.

33. Fraser, *The USA and the Middle East*, pp 38–43.

34. 'The Declaration of the Establishment of the State of Israel, May 14, 1948' , Official Gazette of the 5th Iyar 5708 (14th May 1948), Israel Ministry of Foreign Affairs; http://www.mfa.gov.il/MFA.

35. Weizmann, *Trial and Error*, pp 585–9; Vera Weizmann, *The Impossible Takes Longer*, pp 237–52; R H S Crossman, 'The Prisoner of Rehovoth', in Meyer W

Weisgal and Joel Carmichael (eds), *Chaim Weizmann. A biography by several hands* (Weidenfeld and Nicolson, London: 1962) pp 325–6; Rose, *Chaim Weizmann*, pp 445–59.

36. See T G Fraser, *The Arab-Israeli Conflict*, Third Edition (Palgrave Macmillan, Basingstoke: 2007) pp 195–201; CIA World Factbook, Israel, 2008, https://www.cia.gov/library/publications/the-world-factbook/geos/is.html; http://.un.org/unrwa/publications/index.html.

37. Berlin, *Chaim Weizmann*, pp 42–3.

38. Webster, 'The Founder of the National Home', pp 33–5.

39. Berlin, *Chaim Weizmann*, p 50.

40. 'Dr. Chaim Weizmann's Opening Address to the Israeli Constituent Assembly' (Zionist Federation, London: nd).

Chronology

YEAR	AGE	THE LIFE AND THE LAND
1874		27 Nov: Chaim Weizmann born at Motol.
1882	8	3 May: 'May Laws' enacted in Russia, placing Jews under severe conditions.
1885	11	Weizmann begins secondary education at Pinsk.
1893	19	Weizmann begins university study in Berlin, then Switzerland (doctorate 1899).
1895	21	Dreyfus condemned in France.
1896	22	Theodore Herzl publishes *Der Judenstaat* (The Jews' State)
1898	24	Weizmann attends Second Zionist Congress. Appointed *Privat Dozent* in Chemistry at University of Geneva. Becomes engaged to Sophia Getzova (relationship broken off 1901)
1900	26	Weizmann meets Vera Chatzmann.
1901	27	At Fifth Zionist Congress, Weizmann and Democratic Faction propose a Jewish University.

YEAR	HISTORY	CULTURE
1874	End of Ashanti War.	Thomas Hardy, *Far from the Madding Crowd*.
1882	Triple Alliance between Italy, Germany and Austria-Hungary. British occupy Cairo.	R L Stevenson, *Treasure Island*. Tchaikovsky, '1812 Overture'.
1885	General Gordon killed in fall of Khartoum to the Mahdi.	Gilbert and Sullivan, operetta 'The Mikado'.
1893	Franco-Russian alliance signed. Second Irish Home Rule Bill rejected by House of Lords.	Oscar Wilde, *A Woman of No Importance*. Puccini, opera 'Manon Lescaut'.
1895	Armenians massacred in Ottoman Empire.	H G Wells, *The Time Machine*.
1896	Failure of Jameson Raid. Kaiser Wilhelm II sends 'Kruger Telegram'.	Chekhov, *The Seagull*. Nobel Prizes established.
1898	Dreyfus case: Zola publishes *J'Accuse* letter. Spanish-American War. Death of Bismarck.	Thomas Hardy, *Wessex Poems*. Henry James, *The Turn of the Screw*.
1900	Boxer Rising in China.	Joseph Conrad, *Lord Jim*.
1901	Death of Queen Victoria: Edward VII becomes King. Negotiations for Anglo-German alliance end without agreement.	Rudyard Kipling, *Kim*.

YEAR	AGE	THE LIFE AND THE LAND
1903	29	20 May: Joseph Chamberlain make the Uganda Offer of land for a Jewish settlement; Weizmann opposes it at Sixth Zionist Congress.
1904	30	Weizmann moves to the University of Manchester.
1905	31	Seventh Zionist Congress rejects Uganda Offer.
1906	32	Weizmann meets Arthur Balfour in Manchester. Marries Vera Chatzmann. In France, Dreyfus rehabilitated.
1907	33	Weizmann's first visit to Palestine. Weizmann's first son, Benjamin, born.
1908	34	Establishment of Palestine Office, Jaffa, to purchase land for Jews.
1909	35	Tel Aviv founded.
1914	40	Weizmann meets Herbert Samuel.
1915	41	Weizmann meets David Lloyd George. Begins work on acetone production. Jamal Pasha, Young Turk leader, orders evacuation of Jews from Tel Aviv. Jews deported from Palestine. 25 Apr: Gallipoli campaign begins; Zion Mule Corps employed. 24 Oct: McMahon pledge to Hussein, head of Hashemites, promising support for independence of Arabs. Herbert Samuel circulates Memorandum to parliamentary colleagues proposing Palestine become British Mandate post-war.

YEAR	HISTORY	CULTURE
1903	At its London Congress, the Russian Social Democratic Party splits into Mensheviks and Bolsheviks. Wright Brothers' first flight.	George Bernard Shaw, *Man and Superman.* Film: *The Great Train Robbery.*
1904	Entente Cordiale. Russo-Japanese War.	J M Barrie, *Peter Pan.*
1905	'Bloody Sunday' in Russia.	Edith Wharton, *House of Mirth.*
1906	British ultimatum forces Turkey to cede Sinai Peninsula to Egypt.	John Galsworthy, *A Man of Property.* Invention of first jukebox.
1907	Peace Conference held in The Hague.	Joseph Conrad, *The Secret Agent.*
1908	*The Daily Telegraph* publishes remarks about German hostility towards Britain made by Kaiser Wilhelm II.	Kenneth Grahame, *The Wind in the Willows.*
1909	State visits of Edward VII to Berlin and Rome.	Vasily Kandinksy paints first abstract paintings.
1914	Outbreak of First World War.	Film: Charlie Chaplin in *Making a Living.*
1915	First World War: Battles of Neuve Chapelle and Loos. The 'Shells Scandal'. Germans sink the British liner *Lusitania,* killing 1,198. Germans execute British nurse Edith Cavell in Brussels for harbouring British prisoners.	Joseph Conrad, *Victory.* John Buchan, *The Thirty-Nine Steps.* Ezra Pound, *Cathay.* Duchamp, *The Large Glass.* Pablo Picasso, *Harlequin.* Marc Chagall, *The Birthday.* Max Reger, *Mozart Variations.* Film: *The Birth of a Nation.*

YEAR	AGE	THE LIFE AND THE LAND
1916	42	Weizmann's second son, Michael, is born.
		Sykes-Picot Agreement.
		Arab Revolt
		Lloyd George becomes Prime Minister.
1917	43	Weizmann becomes President of English Zionist Federation.
		Negotiates with British government for pro-Zionist declaration.
		2 Nov: Balfour Declaration issued.
		11 Dec: Allenby enters Jerusalem.
1918	44	Weizmann in Palestine with Zionist Commission; meets Feisal at desert headquarters; lays foundation stone of Hebrew University.
1919	45	3 Jan: Weizmann concludes agreement with Feisal.
		27 Feb: Weizmann addresses Supreme Council at Paris Peace Conference.
		May: American King-Crane Commission to Palestine.

YEAR	HISTORY	CULTURE
1916	First World War: Battles of Verdun and the Somme. US President Woodrow Wilson re-elected.	James Joyce, *Portrait of an Artist as a Young Man.* Film: *Intolerance.*
1917	First World War: USA declares war on Germany. German and Russian delegates sign armistice at Brest-Litovsk.	T S Eliot, *Prufrock and Other Observations.* Film: *Easy Street.*
1918	First World War. German Spring offensives on Western Front fail. Ex-Tsar Nicholas II and family executed. Allied offensives on Western Front have German army in full retreat. Armistice signed between Allies and Germany.	Gerald Manley Hopkins, *Poems.* Luigi Pirandello, *Six Characters in Search of an Author.*
1919	Communist Revolt in Berlin. Treaty of Versailles signed. Irish War of Independence begins. US Senate votes against ratification of Versailles Treaty.	Thomas Hardy, *Collected Poems.* Film: *The Cabinet of Dr Caligari.*

YEAR	AGE	THE LIFE AND THE LAND
1920	46	Mar: Weizmann visits Palestine with his son.
		8 Mar: Syrian Congress proclaims Feisal King of Syria.
		18–26 Apr: Weizmann attends San Remo Conference, when Mandate for Palestine is awarded to Britain.
		30 Jun: Sir Herbert Samuel is appointed High Commissioner and Commander-in-Chief of Palestine.
		Jul: French enter Damascus and expel Feisal from Syria; Weizmann addresses International Zionist Congress in London; President of World Zionist Organisation; quarrels with Brandeis.
1921	47	Apr: Weizmann visits United States.
		Jun: Weizmann attends Zionist Organisation of America Congress in Cleveland.
		23 Aug: Kingdom of Iraq established with Feisal as King. Abdullah is made Emir of Transjordan.
1922	48	Churchill White Paper 'Statement of British Policy in Palestine'.
		24 Jul: League of Nations confirms British Mandate over Palestine.
1925	51	Apr: Weizmann visits Palestine with Balfour for inauguration of Hebrew University.

YEAR	HISTORY	CULTURE
1920	League of Nations comes into existence.	F Scott Fitzgerald, *This Side of Paradise*.
	The Hague is selected as seat of International Court of Justice.	Rambert School of Ballet formed.
	League of Nations moves headquarters to Geneva.	
	Warren G Harding wins US Presidential election.	
	Bolsheviks win Russian Civil War.	
	Government of Ireland Act passed.	
	Adolf Hitler announces his 25-point programme in Munich.	
1921	Irish Free State established.	D H Lawrence, *Women in Love*.
	Peace treaty signed between Russia and Germany.	John Dos Passos, *Three Soldiers*.
	Washington Naval Treaty signed.	Salzburg Festival established.
		Prokofiev, *The Love for Three Oranges*.
1922	Chanak Crisis.	T S Eliot, *The Waste Land*.
	Election in Irish Free State gives majority to Pro-Treaty candidates. IRA takes large areas under its control.	James Joyce, *Ulysses*.
		British Broadcasting Company (later Corporation) (BBC) founded; first radio broadcasts.
1925	Pound Sterling returns to the Gold Standard.	Noel Coward, *Hay Fever*.
	Paul von Hindenburg elected President of Germany.	Film: *Battleship Potemkin*.
	Locarno Treaty signed in London.	

YEAR	AGE	THE LIFE AND THE LAND
1929	55	Formation of Jewish Agency, with Weizmann as President. Arabs attack Jews in Palestine following dispute over Jewish use of Wailing Wall.
1930	56	Passfield White Paper proposes curtailment of Jewish immigration to Palestine; Weizmann resigns as President of Zionist Organisation (he is reappointed in 1935) and Jewish Agency.
1931	57	Feb: Weizmann secures MacDonald Letter in continuing support of Balfour Declaration. Jul: Zionist Congress votes against Weizmann.
1933	59	Beginning of mass immigration of Jews from Europe to Palestine following Hitler's rise to power.
1934	60	Weizmann builds home at Rehovoth and is appointed to post at Daniel Sieff Research Institute.

YEAR	HISTORY	CULTURE
1929	Germany accepts Young Plan at Reparations Conference in the Hague. Allies agree to evacuate the Rhineland. Wall Street crashes.	Ernest Hemingway, *A Farewell to Arms*. Erich Maria Remarque, *All Quiet on the Western Front*.
1930	London Naval Treaty signed. Nazi Party in Germany gains 107 seats in Reichstag.	T S Eliot, *Ash Wednesday*. W H Auden, *Poems*. Noel Coward, *Private Lives*.
1931	National Government formed in Great Britain. Britain abandons Gold Standard. Nazi leader Adolf Hitler and Alfred Hugenberg of the German National Party agree to co-operate.	Architecture: Empire State Building New York. Films: *Dracula. Little Caesar.*
1933	Adolf Hitler appointed Chancellor of Germany. Fire destroys the Reichstag. Enabling Act gives Hitler dictatorial powers. Germany withdraws from League of Nations.	George Orwell, *Down and Out in Paris and London*. Films: *Duck Soup. King Kong. Queen Christina.*
1934	After German President Hindenburg dies, role of President and Chancellor are merged and Hitler becomes *Führer*. USSR admitted to League of Nations. In USSR, Kirov is assassinated.	Robert Graves, *I, Claudius*. Films: *David Copperfield.*

YEAR	AGE	THE LIFE AND THE LAND
1936	62	Arab Revolt.
1937	63	Peel Commission Report proposes partition into independent Arab and Jewish states. Weizmann is converted to partition by Coupland.
1939	65	Attends St James's Palace Conference. Appalled by British White Paper on Palestine proposing independent state and limited Jewish immigration
1942	68	11 Feb: Son Michael killed on active service with RAF. 6–11 May: Weizmann attends Biltmore Conference in New York, which calls for Palestine to be a Jewish Commonwealth
1945	71	Oct: Jewish Revolt against the Mandate.
1946	72	Weizmann resigns presidency of World Zionist Organisation.
1947	73	15 May: United Nations Special Committee on Palestine (UNSCOP) established. 8 Jul: Weizmann testifies before UNSCOP advocating partition. 19 Nov: Weizmann intervenes with Truman over Negev. 29 Nov: Sanction for a Jewish state is given.

YEAR	HISTORY	CULTURE
1936	German troops reoccupy Rhineland. Spanish Civil War.	BBC begins world's first television transmission service.
1937	Coronation of George VI. Italy joins German-Japanese Anti-Comintern Pact.	John Steinbeck, *Of Mice and Men*. Film: *A Star is Born*.
1939	German invasion of Poland. Britain and France declare war. Soviets invade Finland.	Thomas Mann, *Lotte in Weimar*. Films: *Gone with the Wind. The Wizard of Oz*.
1942	Wannsee Conference for Final Solution held in Germany. Rommel defeated at El Alamein. Battle of Stalingrad in USSR.	Enid Blyton publishes the first 'Famous Five' book, *Five on a Treasure Island*. Film: *Casablanca*.
1945	Hitler commits suicide in Berlin, and city surrenders to Soviets. VE Day: 8 May. United Nations Charter is ratified by 29 nations.	Evelyn Waugh, *Brideshead Revisited*. Film: *Brief Encounter*.
1946	Churchill's 'Iron Curtain' speech. Nuremberg Trials establish guilty verdicts for war crimes.	Bertrand Russell, *History of Western Philosophy*. Film: *It's a Wonderful Life*.
1947	'Truman Doctrine' pledges to support 'free peoples resisting subjugation by armed minorities or outside pressures'. US Secretary of State calls for relief aid to Europe. Indian Independence and Partition.	Anne Frank, *The Diary of Anne Frank*. Tennessee Williams, *A Streetcar Named Desire*. Films: *Monsieur Verdoux. Black Narcissus*.

YEAR	AGE	THE LIFE AND THE LAND
1948	74	19 Mar: Weizmann meets Truman for second time.
		14 May: British Mandate ends: State of Israel declared and recognised by USA.
		15 May: Arab League armies attack Israel.
		17 May: Weizmann appointed President of the State of Israel.
1949	75	Jan: Weizmann's presidency confirmed in first Israeli election.
		Feb: First Arab-Israeli war ends.
1952	78	9 Nov: Weizmann dies at Rehovoth.

YEAR	HISTORY	CULTURE
1948	Gandhi assassinated. Berlin Airlift. Truman wins US Presidential Election.	Graham Greene, *The Heart of the Matter*. Olympic Games held in London. Film: *The Fallen Idol. Hamlet. Whisky Galore.* Radio: *Take It From Here. Mrs Dale's Diary.*
1949	Foundation of North Atlantic Treaty Organisation (NATO). Berlin blockade is lifted. Mao Zedong establishes People's Republic of China.	George Orwell, *Nineteen Eighty-Four*. Film: *The Third Man.*
1952	Death of King George VI: succeeded by Queen Elizabeth II. Mau-Mau Rising in Kenya.	Agatha Christie, *The Mousetrap*. Film: *High Noon.*

Further Reading

The student of Weizmann is fortunate in many respects. The essential starting point for any study of his life and career is his autobiography, *Trial and Error*, which he published in 1949 (Hamish Hamilton, London: 1949). Book One, which covers the period down to the Balfour Declaration, was finished in 1941; Book Two, which takes his story down to November 1947, was completed that year; and in 1948 he wrote an Epilogue. The autobiography is full of fascinating insights, not least into his early life in Tsarist Russia and the formative years of the Zionist movement, but it sometimes strays over dates and the sequence of events. Shortly before her death in September 1966, Vera Weizmann recounted her memoirs to David Tutaev, and these were published the following year as *The Impossible takes Longer* (Hamish Hamilton, London: 1967). It is full of sharp observations, as well as valuable extracts from her diary.

The Letters and Papers of Chaim Weizmann are the rock on which any study of his career must be based. Under the General Editorship of Weizmann's friend and colleague, Meyer W Weisgal, and the auspices of the Weizmann Archives in Rehovoth, the first volume in the series, edited by

Leonard Stein, appeared in 1968 (Oxford University Press), and covered the years down to 1902. Twenty-two subsequent volumes of letters appeared under the hand of different editors, but the editorial work was uniformly outstanding, and the notes scholarly and invaluable. Few 20th-century leaders have left such a record. Especially illuminating are the letters he wrote to his wife during his frequent periods of absence. Of fundamental importance to this study have been: Leonard Stein, editor, Volume VII, Series A, August 1914–November 1917 (Oxford University Press, Israel Universities Press: 1975); Dvorah Barzilay and Barnet Livinoff, editors, Volume VIII, Series A, November 1917–October 1918 (Transaction Books, Rutgers University, Israel Universities Press: 1977); Jehuda Reinharz, editor, Volume IX, Series A, October 1918–July 1920 (Transaction Books, Rutgers University, Israel Universities Press: 1977). Weizmann's appearance before the Paris Peace Conference may be studied in M Dockrill (ed), *British Documents on Foreign Affairs: Reports and Papers from the Foreign Office Confidential Print*, Part II, Series I, *The Paris Peace Conference of 1919*, Volume 2, *Supreme Council Minutes, January-March 1919* (University Publications of America: 1989).

Weizmann has been well served by his biographers. *Chaim Weizmann. A Tribute on his Seventieth Birthday*, edited by Paul Goodman (Victor Gollancz, London: 1945), contains reminiscences, appropriately reverential, from a number of colleagues, and a particularly valuable section on his scientific work. An even more useful collaborative work is *Chaim Weizmann. A biography by several hands*, edited by Meyer W Weisgal and Joel Carmichael (Weidenfeld and Nicolson, London: 1962). In 1976, Barnet Litvinoff published a well-written overview, *Weizmann. Last of the Patriarchs* (Hodder and Stoughton, London: 1976). Norman Rose wrote a masterly account in *Chaim Weizmann. A Biography* (Weidenfeld and Nicolson, London: 1987). It is replete with insights. Finally, there are the two magisterial volumes by Jehuda Reinharz: *Chaim Weizmann. The Making of a Zionist Leader* (Oxford University Press, Oxford: 1985), covering his life down to 1914, which was followed by *Chaim Weizmann. The Making of a Statesman* (Oxford University Press, Oxford: 1993), which continued the story down to 1922. My debt to these works, and especially to those of Rose and Reinharz, will be obvious.

Four published lectures on Weizmann by his friends and contemporaries also give valuable insights. In 1955, the British international historian and veteran of the Paris Peace Conference, Sir Charles Webster, delivered 'The Chaim Weizmann Memorial Lecture' on *The Founder of the National Home*, subsequently published by the Yad Chaim Weizmann. The next year, Weizmann's American colleague, Louis Lipsky, continued with 'The Chaim Weizmann Memorial Lecture' on *Herzl, Weizmann and the Jewish State* (Yad Chaim Weizmann, n.d.: c1957). The 1958 Herbert Samuel Lecture at Hebrew University was given by the eminent scholar Isaiah Berlin, and published as *Chaim Weizmann* (Herzl Institute: 1958). Finally, in 1960 a lecture given at Rehovoth entitled 'Chaim Weizmann' by the British politician R H S Crossman appeared in the journal *Encounter*. All four repay study.

The standard account of Zionism remains Walter Laqueur, *A History of Zionism* (Schocken Books, New York: 1972, 1989 edition), and for the period under review it can be supplemented by David Vital, *Zionism: The Crucial Phase* (Oxford University Press, Oxford: 1987). Herzl's career is best studied in Alex Bein, *Theodore Herzl. A Biography*, translated by Maurice Samuel (The Jewish Publication Society of America, Philadelphia: 1940), and his thinking in *The Jewish State. An Attempt at a Modern Solution of the Jewish Question*, translated by Sylvie d'Avigdor (H Pordes, London: 1972). Leonard Stein's *The Balfour Declaration* (Valentine, Mitchell, London: 1961) is a classic piece of historical writing, but since he did not then have access to the British records, it should be used together with Isaiah Friedman, *The Question of Palestine, 1914–1918. British-Jewish-Arab Relations* (Routledge and Kegan Paul, London: 1973), who did.

For an Arab perspective on these events, George Antonius, *The Arab Awakening* (Hamish Hamilton, London: 1938) remains indispensable. There is useful information in Philip Mattar, *The Mufti of Jerusalem. Al-Hajj Amin al-Husayni and the Palestinian National Movement* (Columbia University Press, New York: 1988). The British military administration of Palestine is covered, somewhat opaquely, in the memoirs of Ronald Storrs, *Orientations* (Ivor Nicholson and Watson, London: 1939). The *Memoirs of Viscount Samuel* (The Cresset Press, London: 1945) provide his important testimony. Balfour's role is traced in *Arthur James Balfour. First Earl of Balfour*, by his niece Blanche E C Dugdale, two volumes (Hutchinson, London: 1939), especially useful since she became a close friend of Weizmann. There are also worthwhile perspectives in the works of two British Zionist sympathisers: Herbert Sidebotham, *Great Britain and Palestine* (Macmillan, London: 1937); and Trevor Wilson (ed), *The Political Diaries of C. P. Scott 1911–1928* (Collins, London: 1970). There is a mine of information in *Palestine. A Study of Jewish, Arab, and British Policies*, two volumes (Yale University Press, New Haven: 1947). No student of the period can afford to ignore the *Palestine Royal Commission Report*

(Cmd. 5479, 1937), especially since Weizmann adopted its views on partition, which are analysed in T G Fraser, 'A Crisis of Leadership: Weizmann and the Zionist Reactions to the Peel Commission's Proposals, 1937–8', *Journal of Contemporary History*, volume 23, number 4 (October 1988). An alternative perspective on Weizmann can be found in Melvin L Urofsky and David W Levy, *Letters of Louis D. Brandeis*, Volume IV (1916–1921) (State University of New York Press, Albany: 1975). Shabtai Teveth, *Ben-Gurion. The Burning Ground 1886–1948* (Robert Hale, London: 1987) traces, *inter alia*, the relationship between its subject and Weizmann.

The context of Weizmann's appearance before the Peace Conference is set in H W V Temperley (ed), *A History of the Peace Conference of Paris*, volume VI (Oxford University Press, Oxford: 1924, reprinted 1969). For an overview of the Middle East peace settlement, see David Fromkin, *A Peace to End All Peace. Creating the Modern Middle East 1914–1922* (Penguin Books, London: 1991), and see also Alan Sharp, *The Versailles Settlement. Peacemaking After the First World War, 1919–1923* (Palgrave Macmillan, Basingstoke: Second Edition, 2008).

Bibliography

Published official documents

British Documents on Foreign Affairs: Reports and Papers from the Foreign Office Confidential Print, General Editors, Kenneth Bourne and D Cameron Watt, Part II, *From the First to the Second World War*, Series I, *The Paris Peace Conference of 1919*, Editor M Dockrill, Volume 2, *Supreme Council Minutes, January-March 1919* (University Publications of America: 1989).

Correspondence between Sir Henry McMahon and the Sharif Hussein of Mecca, July 1915-March 1916, (Cmd. 5957, London: 1939).

'The Declaration of the Establishment of the State of Israel, May 14, 1948', Official Gazette of the 5th Iyar 5708 (14th May 1948), Israel Ministry of Foreign Affairs; http://www.mfa.gov.il/MFA

Documents on British Foreign Policy 1919–1939, First Series, Volume IV, 1919, E L Woodward and Rohan Butler (eds) (Her Majesty's Stationery Office, London: 1952).

Documents on British Foreign Policy 1919–1939, First Series, Volume VIII, International Conferences on High

Policy, 1920, Rohan Butler and J P T Bury (eds) (Her Majesty's Stationery Office, London: 1958).

Palestine Royal Commission Report, (Cmd. 5479, London: 1937).

Statement of British Policy in Palestine, 3 June 1922, (Cmd. 1700, London: 1922).

Published diaries, letters and memoirs

Amery, L S, *My Political Life*, Volume Two, *War and Peace, 1914–1929* (Hutchinson, London: 1953).

Ben-Gurion, David, *Recollections*, edited by Thomas R Bransten (Macdonald Unit 75, London: 1970).

Bentwich, Norman & Helen, *Mandate Memories 1918–1948* (The Hogarth Press, London: 1965).

'Dr. Chaim Weizmann's Opening Address to the Israeli Constituent Assembly' (Zionist Federation, London: n.d.).

Fraser, T G (ed), *The Middle East, 1914–1979* (Edward Arnold, London: 1980).

Gilbert, Martin, *Winston S. Churchill*, Companion, Volume IV, Parts 2 and 3 (Heinmann, London: 1977).

Goodman, Paul (ed), *Chaim Weizmann. A Tribute on his Seventieth Birthday* (Victor Gollancz Ltd., London: 1945).

Herzl, Theodor, *The Jewish State. An Attempt at a Modern Solution of the Jewish Question* (H Pordes, London: 1972).

Laqueur, Walter (ed), *The Israel-Arab Reader* (Pelican Books, London: 1970).

Lloyd George, David, *War Memoirs*, two-volume edition (Odhams Press Limited, London: 1938).

'Presidential Address by Dr. Chaim Weizmann, Twenty-
Second Zionist Congress, Basle, 9th December 1949',
(The Jewish Agency for Palestine, London: n.d.).

Samuel, The Rt. Hon. Viscount, *Memoirs* (The Cresset
Press, London: 1945).

Storrs, Ronald, *Orientations* (Ivor Nicholson & Watson
Ltd, London: 1939).

Urofsky, Melvin L, and Levy, David W (eds), *Letters of
Louis D. Brandeis*, Volume IV (1916–1921) (State
University of New York Press, Albany: 1975).

Weisgal, Meyer W (General Editor), *The Letters and Papers
of Chaim Weizmann*, Series A, Letters: Leonard Stein
(ed), Volume I (Oxford University Press, London: 1968);
Leonard Stein (ed), Volume VII (Oxford University
Press, London and New York: 1975); Dvorah Barzilay
and Barnet Litvinoff (eds), Volume VIII (Transaction
Books, Rutgers University, Israel Universities Press,
Jerusalem: 1977); Jehuda Reinharz (ed), Volume
IX (Transaction Books, Rutgers University, Israel
Universities Press, Jerusalem: 1977); http://www.mfa.gov.
il/MFA; Camillo Dresner (ed), Volume XIV (Transaction
Books, Rutgers University, Israel Universities Press,
Jerusalem: 1978).

Weizmann, Chaim, *Trial and Error. The Autobiography of
Chaim Weizmann* (Hamish Hamilton, London: 1949).

Weizmann, Vera, *The Impossible Takes Longer. Memoirs
by the wife of Israel's First President as told to David
Tutaev* (Hamish Hamilton, London: 1967).

Wilson, Sir Arnold T, MP, *Loyalties. Mesopotamia*, Volume
II, 1917–1920, *A Personal and Historical Record*
(Oxford University Press, London: 1931).

Wilson, Trevor (ed), *The Political Diaries of C. P. Scott 1911–1928* (Collins, London: 1928).

Biographies

Bein, Alex, *Theodore Herzl* (The Jewish Publication Society of America, Philadelphia: 1941).

Berlin, Isaiah, *Chaim Weizmann* (Herzl Institute Pamphlet No 8, New York: 1958).

Dugdale, Blanche E C, *Arthur James Balfour. First Earl of Balfour* (Hutchinson, London: 1936).

Litvinoff, Barnet, *Weizmann. Last of the Patriarchs* (Hodder and Stoughton, London: 1976).

Marlowe, John, *Late Victorian, The Life of Sir Arnold Wilson* (The Cresset Press, London: 1967).

Mattar, Philip, *The Mufti of Jerusalem. Al-Hajj Amin Al-Husayni and the Palestinian National Movement* (Columbia University Press, New York, 1988).

Reinharz, Jehuda, *Chaim Weizmann. The Making of a Zionist Leader* (Oxford University Press, New York and Oxford: 1985).

——, *Chaim Weizmann. The Making of a Statesman* (Oxford University Press, Oxford and New York: 1993).

Rose, Norman, *Chaim Weizmann. A Biography* (Weidenfeld and Nicolson, London: 1986).

Teveth, Shabtai, *Ben-Gurion. The Burning Ground 1886–1948* (Robert Hale Limited, London: 1987).

Webster, Sir Charles Kingsley, *The Founder of the National Home* (Yad Chaim Weizmann, Rehovoth: 1955).

Weisgal, Meyer W, and Joel Carmichael, *Chaim Weizmann. A Biography by Several Hands*, (Weidenfeld and Nicolson, London: 1962).

Secondary Sources

Adams, Frank, 'Palestine Agriculture', in *Palestine: A Decade of Development. The Annals of the American Academy of Political and Social Science* (November 1932).

Antonius, George, *The Arab Awakening* (Librairie du Liban, Beirut: 1969, original edition Hamish Hamilton, London: 1938).

Bosco, Andrea, and May, Alex (eds), *The Round Table, the Empire/Commonwealth and British Foreign Policy* (Lothian Foundation Press, London: 1997).

Dunn, Seamus, and Fraser, TG (eds), *Europe and Ethnicity. The First World War and contemporary ethnic conflict* (Routledge, London: 1996).

Esco Foundation for Palestine, *Palestine. A Study of Jewish, Arab and British Policies* (Yale University Press, New Haven: 1947).

Fraser, T G, *Partition in Ireland, India and Palestine: theory and practice* (Macmillan, London and Basingstoke: 1984).

——, *The USA and the Middle East since World War 2* (Macmillan, Basingstoke and London: 1989).

——, *The Arab-Israeli Conflict*, Third Edition (Macmillan, Basingstoke: 2007).

Friedman, Isaiah, *The Question of Palestine 1914–1918. British-Jewish-Arab Relations* (Routledge and Kegan Paul, London: 1973).

Fromkin, David, *A Peace to End All Peace. Creating the Modern Middle East 1914–1922* (Penguin Books, London: 1989).

Hourani, Albert, *A History of the Arab Peoples* (The Belknap Press of Harvard University Press, Cambridge, Massachusetts: 1991).

Jeffery, Keith, *The British Army and the Crisis of Empire 1918–22* (Manchester University Press, Manchester: 1984).

Kressel, Getzel, 'Zionist Congresses', Israel Pocket Library, *Zionism* (Keter Publishing House, Jerusalem: 1973).

Laqueur, Walter: *A History of Zionism* (Schocken Books, New York: 1989).

Pappe, Ilan, *A History of Modern Palestine. One Land, Two Peoples* (Cambridge University Press, Cambridge: 2004).

Sachar, Howard M, *A History of Israel. From the Rise of Zionism to Our Time* (Basil Blackwell, Oxford: 1976).

Sharp, Alan, *The Versailles Settlement. Peacemaking After the First World War, 1919–1923* (Palgrave Macmillan, Basingstoke: Second Edition, 2008).

Shlaim, Avi, *The Iron Wall. Israel and the Arab World* (Penguin Books, London: 2000).

Slutsky, Dr Yehuda, 'Under Ottoman Rule (1880–1917)', Israel Pocket Library, *History from 1880* (Keter Publishing House, Jerusalem: 1973).

Stein, Leonard, *The Balfour Declaration*, (The Magnes Press, The Hebrew University, The Jewish Chronicle Publications, Jerusalem, London: 1983, original edition 1961).

Tibawi, A L, *A Modern History of Syria including Lebanon and Palestine* (Macmillan, London: 1969).

Vital, David, *Zionism: The Crucial Phase* (Clarendon Press, Oxford: 1987).

Picture Sources

The author and publishers wish to express their thanks to the following sources of illustrative material and/or permission to reproduce it. They will make proper acknowledgements in future editions in the event that any omissions have occurred.

Topham Picturepoint: pp x, 64 and 94.

Endpapers

The Signing of Peace in the Hall of Mirrors, Versailles, 28th June 1919 by Sir William Orpen (Imperial War Museum: akg Images)

Front row: Dr Johannes Bell (Germany) signing with Herr Hermann Müller leaning over him

Middle row (seated, left to right): General Tasker H Bliss, Col E M House, Mr Henry White, Mr Robert Lansing, President Woodrow Wilson (United States); M Georges Clemenceau (France); Mr David Lloyd George, Mr Andrew Bonar Law, Mr Arthur J Balfour, Viscount Milner, Mr G N Barnes (Great Britain); Prince Saionji (Japan)

Back row (left to right): M Eleftherios Venizelos (Greece);

Dr Afonso Costa (Portugal); Lord Riddell (British Press); Sir George E Foster (Canada); M Nikola Pašić (Serbia); M Stephen Pichon (France); Col Sir Maurice Hankey, Mr Edwin S Montagu (Great Britain); the Maharajah of Bikaner (India); Signor Vittorio Emanuele Orlando (Italy); M Paul Hymans (Belgium); General Louis Botha (South Africa); Mr W M Hughes (Australia)

Jacket images

(Front): Topham Picturepoint.

(Back): *Peace Conference at the Quai d'Orsay* by Sir William Orpen (Imperial War Museum: akg Images).

Left to right (seated): Signor Orlando (Italy); Mr Robert Lansing, President Woodrow Wilson (United States); M Georges Clemenceau (France); Mr David Lloyd George, Mr Andrew Bonar Law, Mr Arthur J Balfour (Great Britain); Left to right (standing): M Paul Hymans (Belgium); Mr Eleftherios Venizelos (Greece); The Emir Feisal (The Hashemite Kingdom); Mr W F Massey (New Zealand); General Jan Smuts (South Africa); Col E M House (United States); General Louis Botha (South Africa); Prince Saionji (Japan); Mr W M Hughes (Australia); Sir Robert Borden (Canada); Mr G N Barnes (Great Britain); M Ignacy Paderewski (Poland)

Index

NB All family relations are
to Chaim Weizmann unless
otherwise stated.

A
Ahad Ha'am (Asher Zvi
    Ginsberg) 11, 39
Ahmed Jamal Pasha 41–2,
    47
al-Arif, Arif 99, 113
al-Husayni, Haj Amin 87,
    99, 113, 132
al-Husayni, Musa Kasim
    99, 116
al-Jamal, Shibly 116
Allenby, General Sir
    Edmund 47, 67, 68, 70,
    85, 86, 90, 125
Amery, Leo 50, 61, 129
anti-Semitism 8–10, 59, 136
Arab Revolt (1916), the 47

Asquith, Herbert 37, 39,
    40–1, 43, 49

B
Baker, Philip Noel 90
Balfour, Arthur James
    17–18, 37, 39, 40–1, 43,
    49, 54–62, 70, 72, 74, 76,
    83, 85, 86, 89–91, 100,
    101, 103, 111, 115–16,
    119, 124, 125–6, 145,
    146
    Weizmann, and, 17–18,
        54, 60, 70, 85, 91–2,
        125
Balfour Declaration, the
    49, 51, 57–63,, 67, 68, 73,
    76–7, 88–9, 98, 100–2,
    106–7, 111, 115–22, 128
Beeley, Harold 137
Begin, Menachem 43

Ben-Gurion, David 31, 42,
    103–6, 115, 124, 133, 135,
    137–40, 142–3, 146
Ben Yehuda, Eliezer 32
Bentwich, Joseph 53
Berthelot, Philippe 100–2
Bevin, Ernest 137
'Biltmore Program', the 137,
    139
Birnbaum, Nathan 8, 11
Bols, Major-General Sir
    Louis 107–8
Brandeis, Louis B 20, 55,
    59–62, 69, 71, 106,
    111–13, 115, 134, 146
    Weizmann, and 55,
        59–61, 71, 106–7,
        111–13, 134
Bryce, Lord 70
Bunsen, Sir Maurice de 43,
    46
Bystrzycki, Professor 7, 11

C
Cambon, Jules 54, 60
Camp, Major J N 87
Cecil, Lord Robert 50,
    54–5, 58–9, 63, 70, 72, 90
Chamberlain, Austen 129
Chamberlain, Joseph 124
Chamberlain, Neville 124,
    134

Churchill, Winston 18, 41,
    48, 110, 114–18, 120, 124,
    133, 146
Churchill White Paper, the
    120–1
Clayton, General Sir
    Gilbert 45, 68, 69, 72, 86,
    90
Clemenceau, Georges 77–9,
    88
Cohen, Robert Waley 19
Cornwallis, Lieutenant-
    Colonel 86
Coupland, Reginald 50,
    132–3
Cowen, Joseph 53, 68
Cox, Sir Percy 110
Curzon, Lord 61, 62, 86–7,
    89–90, 100–1, 103, 129,
    145

D
Dizengoff, Meir 32
Dreyfus, Captain Alfred 9
Dreyfus, Charles 17
Drummond, Sir Eric 85

E
Eden, Anthony 134
Eder, Dr David 68, 71
Egypt 42, 44, 55, 68, 98,
    108, 125, 137

El Arish Offer, the 14, 76
Exodus 1947 (refugee ship)
139

F

Feisal, Emir 47, 69, 71,
73–4, 84–8, 98–9, 103,
109–10, 123, 145
Weizmann, and 69–70,
73–4, 84–8, 145
Feisal-Weizmann
Agreement, the 69, 73–4
First World War, the 33–5,
36–7, 41–2, 44–8, 51, 67
France 37, 40, 43, 77, 100
Middle-Eastern interests
46–7, 54–5, 84, 90,
102
Frankfurter, Felix 84, 112,
134
French, Colonel John 90
Friedman, Rabbi David 6,
11

G

Gaster, Sir Moses 53
George V, King 68
Germany 7, 9, 20, 26, 31,
34, 36–7, 40, 97, 131–2,
135
Jews, and the 42, 57, 60,
131, 136

Goldsmid, Osmond
d'Avigdor 19
Gouraud, General Henri
109
Graham, Sir Ronald 57, 90
Great Britain
Middle-Eastern interests
36–9, 43, 45–7
Palestine Mandate 75–7,
79, 85–7, 89, 90,
102–3, 117–22, 137–8
Zionism, and 38–41,
48–9, 51–5, 58–9,
70–1, 128–9
Greenberg, Leopold 14, 19,
52
Grey, Sir Edward 37

H

Haas, Jacob de 75, 78,
112
Hankey, Maurice 115
Haycraft, Sir Thomas 114,
119
Hebrew language 32, 34
Hebrew University 13, 33–4,
43, 70, 72, 111, 124
Herzl, Theodore 8–11, 12,
14–15, 18, 32, 133, 146
Hibbat Zion movement 4,
6, 12, 30
Hitler, Adolf 9, 131, 135

Hogarth, Commander
    David 70
Hope Simpson, Sir John
    128–9
House, Colonel Edward M
    59, 60–1, 74
Hussein, Sherif 44–7

I

India 37, 62, 108–9, 139
Iraq 25, 102, 108–10,
    115–16, 125
Ireland 27, 108, 118, 120, 132
Israel 31, 142–4
Italy 11, 77, 78–9, 97, 100,
    132

J

Jabotinsky, Vladimir 42–3,
    53, 99, 113, 146
Jacobson, Eddie 142
Japan 77, 78, 100, 132
Jerusalem 8, 13, 18, 21, 24,
    27, 28–30, 33, 46, 67, 68,
    87, 90, 99–100, 107–8,
    110, 113–15, 133, 138, 140
Johnson, Robert
    Underwood 100

K

King-Crane Commission,
    the 88

L

Lansing, Robert 78, 82, 84,
    120
Lawrence, T E 47, 70, 73–4,
    109
League of Nations, the 76,
    79, 101, 117, 122, 126
Levi, Sylvain 68, 78, 81, 83,
    84, 146
Levi-Bianchini, Angelo 67
Lloyd George, David 38–41,
    48–9, 54, 57, 58, 60, 71,
    78, 85, 88, 90, 100, 101,
    102 103, 115–16, 120,
    121, 123, 127, 133, 145,
    146
Lueger, Dr Karl 9

M

MacDonald, Malcolm 135
MacDonald, Ramsay 123,
    127–30
Mack, Julian 75, 112
Magnes, Dr Judah 125
Magnus, Sir Philip 19
Makino, Baron 78
Malcolm, James 52
Matsui, Mr 100–1
McMahon, Sir Henry 44–6
McMahon Letter, the 45–6
Millerand, Alexandre
    100–1

Milner, Alfred Lord 49–50,
58–9, 61, 78
Mond, Sir Alfred 70
Money, General Sir Arthur
75, 86
Montagu, Edwin 40, 57,
58–62, 118, 146
Montefiore, Claude 19
Morgenthau, Henry 42, 56

N
Nathan, Sir Frederick 48
Nitti, Francesco 100–2

O
Ormsby-Gore, William 50,
56, 63, 68, 69, 70, 79, 133,
134, 135
Ottoman Empire, the 21,
25–8, 34, 36–7

P
Palestine 10–11, 19, 21–35
Arabs 24–8, 68–9, 86–8,
98–9, 110–11, 113–19,
125, 128–9, 135–6
Jewish settlement 24,
30–2, 34–5, 52–3,
57–9, 72–4, 84, 103,
120–1, 124, 131–2, 135
Mandate 46–7, 75, 85–91,
102–3, 106, 109,

115–22, 126, 128, 130,
133, 138–42
partition of 12, 55,
132–4, 138–42
Palestine Arab Congress,
the 116–17
Paris Peace Conference, the
77–85
Zionist delegation at
78–83
Passfield, Lord 127–9
Passfield White Paper, the
129–30
Patterson, Lieutenant-
Colonel John Henry 42
Perkin, Professor William
Henry 16, 19, 20
Pichon, Stephen 63, 78–9
Picot, François Georges
46
Plumer of Messines, Field-
Marshal Lord 125

R
Reading, Lord 70, 127
Rothschild, Baron Edmond
de 30
Rothschild, James de 53
Rothschild, Leopold de 19
Rothschild, Lord 53, 56–60,
62, 63, 75, 81
Ruppin, Dr Arthur 32, 33

Russia 3–7, 15, 41, 43, 47,
    51, 62, 63, 67, 127
    pogroms 13–14, 99

S
Sacher, Harry 53
Samuel, Herbert 37–9,
    40–1, 45, 49, 53, 58, 63,
    70, 72, 86, 89, 91, 100,
    102–3, 107, 113, 114–15,
    117–19, 121, 124–5, 133
San Remo Conference, the
    97, 99–100, 103, 108, 110,
    114, 116, 145
Scott, C P 38–41, 48, 54,
    71
Second World War, the
    136–7
Sharett, Moshe 143
Shaw, Sir Walter 126–7
Sidebotham, Herbert 58
Silver, Rabbi Abba Hillel
    136, 148
Simon, Leon 68
Smuts, General Jan 58, 70,
    128, 129
Sokolovsky, Shlomo 4
Sokolow, Nahum 13, 20,
    52–4, 57, 60, 63, 70, 75,
    78–9, 81, 89
Sonnino, Baron 78
Spire, André 78, 81

'Statement of the Zionist
    Oganisation regarding
    Palestine' 75–7, 79
Storrs, Colonel Ronald 68,
    90
Sykes, Sir Mark 46, 50–3,
    56, 63, 70, 123
Sykes-Picot Agreement, the
    46–7, 50, 54–5
Syria 21, 41, 44, 46, 70, 74,
    86, 88, 90–1, 98, 101–2,
    109–10, 125, 134
Szold, Robert 113, 134

T
Tardieu, André 84
Tel Aviv 11, 32–3, 42, 68,
    71, 124, 125, 132, 144
Truman, Harry S 140–3, 145
Trumpeldor, Joseph 42, 98

U
'Uganda Offer', the 14–15,
    17, 76
United Nations Special
    Committee on Palestine
    139
United States of America,
    the 5, 20, 55–7, 59, 61–3,
    67, 71, 74, 77–8, 80, 86,
    88, 97, 106–7, 111–13,
    137, 140–2

Ussishkin, Menahem
Mendel 12, 15, 20, 78, 81,
111, 112, 134, 146

V
Vansittart, Robert 97, 100
Vatican, the 25, 101, 119
Versailles, Treaty of 97, 131

W
Wedgwood, Josiah 40
Weisgal, Meyer 137
Weizmann, Benjamin (son)
16
Weizmann, Chaim
acetone production, and
47–9
Balfour, and 17–18, 54,
60, 70, 85, 91–2, 115,
125
Balfour Declaration, and
the 38–41, 49, 52–63
Ben-Gurion, and 31,
103–6, 124, 137, 138,
143–4
Biltmore Program, and
the 137, 139
Brandeis, and 55, 59–61,
71, 106–7, 111–13, 134
Churchill White Paper,
and the 120–1
death 144

Democratic Faction 12,
33
early life 3–7
Feisal, and 69–70, 73–4,
84–8, 145
Hebrew University, and
13, 33–4, 43, 70, 72,
111
Manchester, in 15–20,
38
Palestine, visits to 19,
21–35, 67–70, 91–2,
111, 124–5
Paris Peace Conference,
at the 74–83
Passfield White Paper,
and the 129–30
President of Israel 142–4
San Remo Conference, at
the 97–102
scientific career 7, 13,
15–16, 19
Technikum, and the 34
Weizmann, Michael (son)
16, 136
Weizmann, Ozer (father)
3–4
Weizmann, Rachel Leah
(mother) 4
Weizmann, Vera (wife) 13,
16, 20, 68–9, 92, 100, 102
Wilson, Arnold T 108, 110

Wilson, Woodrow 55, 59–60, 61, 74, 78, 88, 90, 101, 109
Wingate, Sir Reginald 68
Wise, Stephen 75, 112, 134
Wolfssohn, David 15, 20
Woodhead, Sir John 134–5

Z

Zion Mule Corps, the 42
Zionism, origins of 7–13
Zionist Commission, the 67–9, 72, 78, 80, 88

Zionist Congresses:
  First 10–12, 141
  Second 12
  Fifth 12, 33
  Sixth 14–15
  Seventh 15
  Eleventh 33
  Sixteenth 126
  Twenty-second 138
Zionist Organisation of America, the 76, 111–13

Makers
of the
Modern
World

UK PUBLICATION: November 2008 to December 2010
CLASSIFICATION: Biography/History/
    International Relations
FORMAT: 198 × 128mm
EXTENT: 208pp
ILLUSTRATIONS: 6 photographs plus 4 maps
TERRITORY: world

Chronology of life in context, full index, bibliography innovative layout
with sidebars

Woodrow Wilson: United States of America by Brian Morton
Friedrich Ebert: Germany by Harry Harmer
Georges Clemenceau: France by David Watson
David Lloyd George: Great Britain by Alan Sharp
Prince Saionji: Japan by Jonathan Clements
Wellington Koo: China by Jonathan Clements
Eleftherios Venizelos: Greece by Andrew Dalby
From the Sultan to Atatürk: Turkey by Andrew Mango
The Hashemites: The Dream of Arabia by Robert McNamara
Chaim Weizmann: The Dream of Zion by Tom Fraser
Piip, Meierovics & Voldemaras: Estonia, Latvia & Lithuania by Charlotte Alston
Ignacy Paderewski: Poland by Anita Prazmowska
Beneš, Masaryk: Czechoslovakia by Peter Neville
Károlyi & Bethlen: Hungary by Bryan Cartledge
Karl Renner: Austria by Jamie Bulloch
Vittorio Orlando: Italy by Spencer Di Scala
Pašić & Trumbić: The Kingdom of Serbs, Croats and Slovenes by Dejan Djokic
Aleksandŭr Stamboliĭski: Bulgaria by R J Crampton
Ion Bratianu: Romania by Keith Hitchin
Paul Hymans: Belgium by Sally Marks
General Smuts: South Africa by Antony Lentin
William Hughes: Australia by Carl Bridge
William Massey: New Zealand by James Watson
Sir Robert Borden: Canada by Martin Thornton
Maharajah of Bikaner: India by Hugh Purcell
Afonso Costa: Portugal by Filipe Ribeiro de Meneses
Epitácio Pessoa: Brazil by Michael Streeter
South America by Michael Streeter
Central America by Michael Streeter
South East Asia by Andrew Dalby
The League of Nations by Ruth Henig
Consequences of Peace: The Versailles Settlement – Aftermath and Legacy
    by Alan Sharp